I take great pleasure in applauding the advent of the Ubu Repertory Theater Publications. Devoted to bringing English versions of important contemporary dramatic works from French-speaking countries, this program could not be more important or timely when institutions such as the Eugene O'Neill Theater Center and the Milwaukee Repertory Theater have begun to embrace and espouse the cause of this key element of cultural exchange.

It is particularly important to realize that the plays chosen for translation and publication are not part of any specific genre, but rather are eclectic and are selected to inform the English-speaking public of the scope and richness of present-day French-speaking playwrights.

I cherish the hope that this marvelous project will spark a renaissance in professional collaboration between our French and English-speaking theaters and foster greater understanding between diverse national groups.

George C. White, President
Eugene O'Neill Memorial Theater Center

UBU REPERTORY THEATER PUBLICATIONS

Other titles:

1. Yves Navarre, <u>Swimming Pools at War</u>

2. Bernard-Marie Koltès,
   <u>Night Just Before the Forest</u>
   <u>Struggle of the Dogs and the Black</u>

3. Michel Tournier, <u>The Fetishist</u>

4. Jean-Paul Aron, <u>The Office</u>

JEAN-PAUL WENZEL

FAR FROM HAGONDANGE
Translated from the French by Françoise Kourilsky and Nicholas Kepros

VATER LAND,
THE COUNTRY OF OUR FATHERS
by Jean-Paul Wenzel and Bernard Bloch
Translated from the French by Timothy Johns

Ubu Repertory Theater Publications

ISSN 0738-4009

ISBN 0913745-04-9

CONTENTS

FAR FROM HAGONDANGE

Translated from the French by Françoise Kourilsky and Nicholas Kepros

AUTHOR'S NOTE:

A couple in retirement. He worked as an ironworker all his life. Now he works himself to death building a small workshop, his own factory, where he tries in vain to hide from himself the fact that his life -- his entire life -- has been a failure. In the shadow of her husband, who represents her whole life, his wife -- the housewife -- has longed to fulfill a dream of living in the countryside, with its narrow roads, flowers, trees and chestnuts. All she can do is regret till she dies that she was unable to live this other life, this little postcard happiness.

In this experiment in the theatre of daily life, it seemed important to me to put the "old people," who are so often abandoned by society (and the theatre), on stage and to let them speak. A theatre of daily life, where "reality" is constantly circumvented, where alienation and the repression of all life appear most clearly through a selection of moments where nothing is explicitly stated.

The early scenes of the play are consciously written in what one could call a "naturalistic" mode because I want to establish a relationship between the audience and the characters that comes through recognition. This does not mean identification, but a rapport in which the spectator is drawn to recognize in himself or herself that which is, one might say, "exemplified" by the characters.

Never is it for me a matter of presenting a character or even a story in terms of organic continuity, once the spectator has reached the point of recognition. I proceed by way of breaks and leaps, by concentrating and emphasizing features and "accidental" elements of daily life.

For all these reasons, I think that this "theatre of daily life" -- in the text and also in performance (thanks to the direction and the actors' work) -- escapes naturalism.

Jean-Paul Wenzel

After much deliberation, we decided not to transplant the play to foreign soil, but to keep "Hagondange" -- though the word is certainly difficult to pronounce in English and may sound somewhat strange. It is strange sounding in French as well, and most French people have never heard of this small industrial town in the East of France.

To be consistent with our decision, we also left all the names in their French form. Georges and Marie listen to the operetta The White Horse Inn, which never had the same popularity in Great Britain and America that it had in France. The director may choose to substitute a better-known operetta, such as Rosemarie (which has the advantage of being known in France as well). The director may also want to anglicize the French names, have the actors say Aunt Lucy instead of Aunt Lucienne, or perhaps Mr. Dunbar instead of Mr. Duneton. But, then, where does one stop? To be consistent, the name Hagondange should then be anglicized and changed, say to Haggerston, an invented name which would sound as unfamiliar to an English-speaking audience as Hagondange does to a French one. However, by making these changes, we are gradually transplanting the play to a foreign country, where Georges and Marie can no longer have Limoges china or count in francs.

The songs present yet another problem (with the exception of "Que Sera, Sera," which enjoyed an international success). We have adapted "En passant par la Lorraine" so that it can be sung in English to the original tune. However, another ditty may be invented, as long as it includes the word "Captain" -- a necessary bridge into the dialogue. For Marie's song, "La danseuse est Creole," we rendered the original sequence of ideas in a singable (rumba) form of English.

Françoise Kourilsky
Nicholas Kepros   1979

The first American production of <u>Far From Hagondange</u> (then entitled <u>Far From Harrisburg</u>) was given in Françoise Kourilsky and Nicholas Kepros' translation at La Mama in New York on January 5, 1978 with the following cast:

GEORGES .... Pablo Vela
MARIE .... Maurine Holbert
FRANCOISE .... Gaynor Cote

Directed by Françoise Kourilsky.
Set design and lighting by Alain Chambon
<u>Creole Girl</u> set to music by Amy Rubin

What makes people grow old is, on the one hand, of course, the slow disintegration of the body, and on the other, the way people are treated in our society, in terms of their labor power and nothing else. Basically, society arranges from the beginning to treat a worker as an old person later on. It is interested in productive power and nothing beyond that. An old person is someone who has been deformed since childhood, for profit, and who then, at the end of his life, discovers this mutilation which, in turn, hastens his death.

Jean-Paul Sartre

CHARACTERS

GEORGES, retired, 68

MARIE, his wife, 73

FRANÇOISE, travelling salesperson, 27

The action takes place in a small house in the country.

SCENE ONE

(The kitchen-dining area. GEORGES is cleaning a set of tobacco pipes. MARIE is busy straightening up.)

GEORGES

I wouldn't mind a cup of tea.

MARIE

That's odd ... It's not even time for tea; besides, you never drink it ... Don't you want coffee? It's all made, I can heat it up.

GEORGES

No, coffee's too strong. I feel nervous. I'd like some tea.

MARIE

I'll put the kettle on ... I've only got tea bags.

GEORGES

Oh, that's too bad. I'd have loved a good cup of tea. Ceylon. There's nothing like it.

MARIE

Where did you get that idea? You've never had
Ceylon tea. You've really been acting strange
lately.

GEORGES

From now on, I'm drinking tea! Don't forget
that, when you go shopping.

(PAUSE)

MARIE

By the way, the water heater's not working.
Would you take a look at it?

GEORGES

Yes, yes. Later, after I've had my tea.

MARIE

It's three days since there's been any hot
water. It's annoying when I do the dishes.
And there's a whole pile of laundry.

GEORGES

There's no hurry about the laundry. I'll have
a look at the heater.

(PAUSE)

MARIE

The guarantee ran out last week. It's stupid
— a week earlier and we could've had it fixed

MARIE (cont)

for free. Oh, well, appliances don't choose when they're going to break down... Still, you'd think they'd only built it to last as long as the guarantee. It's possible, you know ... Things aren't built to last any more.

GEORGES

I'll take a look at it. I'm sure it's not a big problem.

MARIE

Do you like your tea strong?

GEORGES

Not too ... I don't know. I read an article on the properties of tea. You have to put in a spoonful of tea per person, and let it sit for five or six minutes; it picks you up, and it makes you less nervous than coffee.

MARIE

That all depends on the person. Tea makes me just as nervous as coffee, and I have to go to the bathroom a lot ... It's bad for you.

GEORGES

That's nonsense. Aunt Lucienne's always drunk
tea, and look how well-preserved she is.
That's her secret.

MARIE

I've hardly ever drunk tea, and I feel fine
... And I'm three years older than Aunt
Lucienne.

GEORGES

It's too hot.

MARIE

Let it cool down.

                    (PAUSE)

GEORGES

I wouldn't mind a little snack.

MARIE

What's got into you today? Tea -- and now you
want to eat, at ten o'clock in the morning.
Can't you wait for lunch?

GEORGES

That's not so unusual, after all. I feel a

GEORGES (cont.)

little hungry ... I need a bite of something.
Anything.

MARIE

There is some bologna left, and a little piece
of cheese.

GEORGES

That'll do.

MARIE

I'm out of bread. I'll have to run to the
village in a little while. I have some
crackers, unsalted.

> (GEORGES makes an annoyed
> gesture.)

Now, for heaven's sake don't get worked up.
It's not good for you. Here's a hard roll
from yesterday. Rolls don't keep. No, it's
like a rock. You'll break your teeth on it.

GEORGES

Bring me some bologna, and some cheese and
crackers. I can't deal with crackers, they
always crumble in my hands ... This tea's not
bad -- it's got flavor ... I didn't think it
would. But buy some Ceylon; that's something
else.

MARIE

Yes, yes.

GEORGES

This bologna is going bad, don't you think?

MARIE

I didn't try it ... No, I don't smell anything.

GEORGES

Yes, there's a little rancid taste right at the end. Go on, try it.

MARIE

I don't feel like bologna at this hour.

GEORGES

It's going to make me sick; I can feel it. You'd better throw it out. I'll have a look at the heater. Bologna doesn't keep, even in the refrigerator. You should know that. With your mania for saving everything, you're going to poison me one day. Where's the screwdriver?

MARIE

But, Georges, it's in your workshop ... of course.

> (GEORGES exits slowly.
> MARIE looks after him,
> shakes her head.)

> (BLACKOUT)

14

SCENE TWO

> (The kitchen-dining area.
> GEORGES is repairing the
> water-heater.)

GEORGES

The inside of this thing is all full of muck.
It really has piled up in one year ... Can't
see a thing, it's so dusty. Aren't there any
instructions with the guarantee? ...
Appliances are getting so complicated these
days. Hand me a rag, would you please;
something must be clogged up ... Ever think
how much dust we breathe in a year ... ? Of
course gas leaves a deposit, but all the same!
Pure country air, my eye! Thank you ... Ow!
... This rag's too thin ... There, I can see a
little better now ... Let's see, let's see.
Something's wrong here -- this thing is loose.
Here it is in the instructions ... Well, they
could've made it clearer. What do they care,
as long as they sell you one! Nothing's built
to last any more! What with their new alloys
... worthless. Have you got a needle or a pin

<u>GEORGES</u> (cont.)

handy? We might have to get someone to fix it

... if this doesn't work. Well, let's try it

... The matches!

<u>MARIE</u>

Be careful.

(BLACKOUT)

SCENE THREE

(The bedroom.)

GEORGES

Did you wind up the clock? I can't sleep.

MARIE

It's the tea. It makes you just as nervous as
coffee. I told you so.

(PAUSE.)

(MARIE checks the alarm.)

GEORGES

Set it for 7:30, tomorrow's Saturday. I ought
to finish setting up the workshop. Monday, I
can finally get to work. It'll make a
beautiful workshop. Nice and clean ... Either
my watch is fast or the clock is slow.

(GEORGES turns on the
radio.)

MARIE

I can't sleep either ... It's too cold to work
in the garden. Could I help you tomorrow?

GEORGES

Out of the question. I keep out of your
kitchen. The workshop is my area. You have
to know your way around in there. It's not
that easy.

> (GEORGES picks up _The
> Reader's Digest_ from the
> night-table.)

'Alcoholemia. A medication with an alcohol
base: an intolerance to alcohol; or, the
presence of alcohol in the blood.'

MARIE

A medication.

GEORGES

No. Intoxication due to the presence of
alcohol in the blood begins at 0.5 per cent.
Between 0.8 and 1.2 per cent the motorist gets
a ticket. Above 1.2 per cent it's a criminal
offence.

Plenty of drivers would get tickets, I can
tell you, if they were caught. You don't have
to drink a lot, you know, to have 0.8 per cent
in your blood.

'Sclerosis ... '

MARIE

My sister died of that. Arteriosclerosis.
Hardening of the arteries.

GEORGES

Yes. 'Ludibrious: capricious; sensual; or
worthy of mockery or jest.'

MARIE

It must be something sensual.

GEORGES

No, it comes from the Latin ludus which
means play, or jest; I didn't know it either.
I'd have guessed like you that it was
something sensual.

        (He laughs.)

'Segregative: a. creating separation; b.
causing dryness; c. confidential.'

MARIE

It comes from segregation. Racial
segregation.

GEORGES

Right. A modern derivation of segregation —
the action of separating groups of human

beings from one another. Ah! So it's not necessarily a question of race ... 'Titanium—' That's a metal.

> (He puts down the magazine.)

What time is it?

MARIE

Almost midnight.

> (PAUSE.)

Three years. Not a sound. You can't recapture time, my poor Georges. We should never have left Hagondange. The country's hard on me ... Always the same landscape, unchanging. You too, I can feel it, you're getting old, my poor Georges. Time passes.

> (She sings quietly.)

Que sera, sera,

Whatever will be, will be

The future's not ours to see,

Que sera, sera, la, la ...

GEORGES

I'm going to sleep. Have you been saving
yogurt cups? They're good for keeping screws.

MARIE

Rest, my little Georges.

(BLACKOUT.)

SCENE FOUR

(The kitchen-dining area. GEORGES is eating. MARIE waits on him, sits to eat from time to time.)

GEORGES

After all, I'm not on a salt-free diet, you know. I've told you a hundred times, it's better to add salt beforehand, while food is cooking. It's in all the cook-books. Except for meat, a butcher told me that. You salt meat afterwards, when you're ready to serve it. That way, it retains the juices. If you like meat rare, that is.

MARIE

It's pot roast. You like it. Adding a little salt is easy. It's awful when you've put too much in to start with. You can always add more, but take it out ... Have a big helping. You're eating less and less.

GEORGES

It's my stomach. I'm all bloated lately. I must be gulping air or something. It's nerves. Nothing serious.

> (GEORGES pours a glass of wine.)

This red table wine is no good. It's all mucked up. Not pure. If you want anything good these days, you have to make it yourself.

MARIE

What's today?

GEORGES

Thursday. Seven-thirty p.m., the twenty-second of September. The trees will be changing their leaves before long.

MARIE

We ought to go into town and shop for Sunday dinner.

GEORGES

There's no hurry. Friday ... Saturday ... Sunday, tick-tock, tick-tock. It passes.

> (He hums.)

GEORGES

It passes, time passes.

Time goes on and on,

We're not here for very long.

Is there any cheese?

MARIE

(Giving him some cheese)
They haven't confirmed yet. I hope they come.
A month without any news.

(PAUSE.)

GEORGES

That's all the cheese there is; you have it,
I'm not hungry. A little pipe to top it all
off, and I'll feel like a prince.

(GEORGES fills his pipe,
reads the television
guide. MARIE eats.)

MARIE

It's eight months now since they came to visit
... since Easter. It's because of Marcel ...
If he hadn't gone on strike, he wouldn't be at
the mill now, and they'd have more free time
... Poor Yvonne.

GEORGES

There's nothing on television. I'm going to
bed. The Digest hasn't come this month:
it's late. Nothing works any more.

> (MARIE, clearing the
> table, breaks a glass)

MARIE

It's nothing -- just a jelly glass.

GEORGES

Yes, but it was mine!

> (GEORGES exits. MARIE
> picks up the bits of
> broken glass.)
>
> (BLACKOUT)

SCENE FIVE

> (The workshop. GEORGES is
> working. MARIE enters.)

MARIE

Come and eat. It's nearly one ... the quiz
show's started.

GEORGES

I've got to finish.

MARIE

You can finish after lunch. You have all the
time in the world.

GEORGES

No! I have to finish now.

MARIE

It's not that important. Come and eat.
You've been hammering on that piece of scrap
iron since seven this morning. You'll make
yourself deaf.

GEORGES

I like iron. I like the sound of the mallet
on iron. I have to finish ... I'll have a

GEORGES (cont.)

rack for my pipes at last ... It'll look nice
in the living-room.

MARIE

You're ruining the little bit of health you
have left. Yesterday it was the rain-gutters
you had to fix. Today it's a pipe-rack. And
you don't eat any more; it won't do.

GEORGES

Bring me my lunch box like old times, I'll eat
here.

MARIE

You're not well. You look so pale. Georges!

GEORGES

It's nothing at all. Leave me alone, I'm
getting behind.

MARIE

I don't understand you any more ... Oh, my
God, the potatoes!

(BLACKOUT)

27

SCENE SIX

> (The kitchen-dining area.
> MARIE is washing dishes.
> GEORGES is installing an
> artificial log fire in
> the fireplace.)

MARIE

And twelve! They're all there -- intact --
they were good quality, these plates. They
haven't changed a bit. Forty-seven years of
service and not one crack. They've seen happy
days, these plates, eh, Georges? Weddings,
baptisms, family dinners. And they'll still
be used. They've taken on value. All these
years. Yvonne likes them a lot, we ought to
mention them in the will ... they're Limoges,
they're worth money.

GEORGES

The plates are there, but now we drink out of
jelly glasses. No more stemware. The good
set is gone. Well, it's all the same to me --
stems or jelly glasses.

MARIE

Yvonne looked pale. She doesn't look happy.
He certainly doesn't do her any good, with his
politics. But Marcel seemed better to me this
time.

GEORGES

She didn't make a good match.

MARIE

She hasn't been lucky, poor thing. Not like
me. She was born on the thirteenth. It
hasn't brought her happiness. It depends on
the person. The month of the Virgin -- I'm
sure that's had a good influence on my life.
Nearly fifty years of happiness. That's a
lot. I've always been happy with you,
Georges.

GEORGES

You know how to talk to a man. Come here, let
me give you a kiss.

> (MARIE wipes her hands,
> crosses to the fireplace
> and embraces GEORGES.)

Me, too; I've been happy, Marie.

> (PAUSE.)

GEORGES (cont.)

Let's try the log fire.

> (He plugs it in. It
> doesn't work.)

Those little red bulbs must not be screwed in
properly. I checked them all, though. See if
there's any current. The power might be off.

> (MARIE tries a light
> switch. It works.)

Then it must be the plug. A bad contact.

> (Finally the fire lights
> up. They look at it for
> a brief moment, holding
> hands.)

MARIE

It looks lovely. You'd think it was a real
log fire. It warms up the room -- makes it
nice and cheerful.

GEORGES

I'm going to put my armchair there. Very
rustic. And I'll make a low table for the
corner.

MARIE

Maybe it would be better if we bought a little
wooden one. It'd go better with the rest of
the room.

GEORGES

With iron you can make something that has real
style. It'll mean a lot of work, of course,
but sheet metal under a mallet can take any
form you like. I'll make legs of wrought
iron.

MARIE

If you want to, but it seems to me that a
wooden table ...

GEORGES

A waste of money. Anyway, you don't put a
wooden table near the fire.

> (PAUSE.)

> (GEORGES looks at MARIE.)

I'm going to take a nap.

MARIE

But wasn't it today that Mr. Duneton was
coming by to bring you that book? I ought to
fix myself up a bit. I'm not properly
dressed.

GEORGES

You're fine the way you are. Don't overdo it.

MARIE

I don't have many occasions to look pretty, so
when someone comes to visit ...

GEORGES

(More and more eager)

I've never stopped you from looking pretty for
me.

MARIE

Leave me alone. With your damned country
life, we never see anyone any more; even the
children hardly ever come to see us; as for
quiet, we certainly have our fill of it ...
Why did we ever leave Hagondange?

GEORGES

Don't work yourself up. Come and lie down
with me. You need a rest.

MARIE

You know very well I don't take naps. We're
past the age for that.

GEORGES

Nonsense, age has nothing to do with it. God
won't object. You're still pretty, Marie.
Come and take a little nap.

MARIE

It's not because of God. I just don't care
for it. That's all. I never did .. Let's
change the subject; this embarrasses me.

GEORGES

You don't have the right to refuse, after all
these years; it's true, since I retired I
think about it more. But then we have a lot
more time than we used to. I still want you,
Marie.

(He tries to caress her.)

MARIE

Leave me alone ... I can't ... Mr. Duneton
might arrive any minute, and I have to finish
your cardigan.

(GEORGES exits, slamming
the door. MARIE weeps.)

(BLACKOUT)

SCENE SEVEN

> (The workshop. GEORGES is
> working, building the low
> metal table. He is
> singing.)

GEORGES

Through Lorraine I went a-walking, in my
wooden clogs, Through Lorraine I went
a-walking, in my wooden clogs, When I met
three captains talking, And my clogs they went
pa-pa-pa, la, la, la, etc. Captain ... At
your command, Captain ... Captain, I'm getting
married ... Good luck, old chap ... What shit
... Jules got pulled through the rollers, Boss
... It went crack ... Where are the 25 bolts?
Let's see. Third row, sixth yogurt cup. Ah,
what organization! Nothing left to chance.
All in order ... You're shaking, old man ...
And Fernand and Louis .. Six feet under ...
Dead for their country ... no more poker.
Little table, I'll make you immortal ...
Yvonne ... The furnaces are out, the big
furnaces are out ... Things are going to

change, lads ... The table's rickety. Nothing
works any more ... If at first you don't
succeed, try, try again ... You remember your
moral lesson very well, Georges. Follow his
example, he's going to go a long way ...
Sixty-nine years ... With rubber tips on the
legs, it won't even make any noise ... There's
no more noise, here ... An ideal place for you
to rest ... It's really very quiet here ...
Thank you, sir, thank you very much.

> (He hits the table
> violently with the
> hammer, continues to
> strike as he speaks.)

Stop that racket, for God's sake! It's the
crane, Boss, can't help it ...

> (He sings.)

Put your earplugs in, old buddy,

When you take your nap --

> (He laughs.)

What are we doing here, Marie, what are we
doing?

GEORGES (cont.)

>   (He stops hammering, looks
>   at the table, which is
>   all bashed in.)

It's nothing, Boss ... We'll fix it.

>   (GEORGES goes back to
>   work.)

>   (BLACKOUT)

SCENE EIGHT

(The kitchen—dining area,
near the fireplace.
MARIE is knitting.
GEORGES smokes his pipe.)

MARIE

All the walnuts have dropped off the tree in
the garden. Most of them are already rotten.
It's a pity.

GEORGES

We don't eat them any more, anyhow. We've
even got some left from last year. Just as
well, let 'em rot. Anyway, they won't go to
waste ... With that gang of kids prowling
around. They've pulled up one of the
fence-posts ... I'll have to keep an eye on
'em next time.

MARIE

I've nearly finished your cardigan. Do you
like it?

GEORGES

I really need a work-shirt. My overalls are
worn out, and my grey shirt's torn.

MARIE

We could gather them up and sell them. It'd
help out the kitty ... Did you read Yvonne's
letter? ... My daughter ... You never know
what she's thinking.

GEORGES

It's none of our business ... What time is it?

MARIE

Quarter to two.

GEORGES

I won't have time to finish before dark.

MARIE

But Georges, your tea.

> (She goes to the window.)

The last rose has faded.

> (She goes to find a broom;
> She sings as she sweeps.)

The Creole girl is dancing,

The boys stand all apart;

They all find her entrancing,

But no one knows her heart.

<u>MARIE</u> (cont.)

>Her little foot moves here,
>
>Her little foot moves there,
>
>la, la, la, la...
>
>A smile to this one here,
>
>A glance to that one there,
>
>And it's your turn ...

>>(BLACKOUT)

> (At the door of the
> kitchen—dining area.
> MARIE and FRANÇOISE, a
> traveling salesperson.)

FRANÇOISE

I am making a survey on household appliances

and their use in country living. I see you

have every comfort here. May I ask you a few

questions? It won't take long.

MARIE

Certainly ... sit down.

FRANÇOISE

Do you live alone?

MARIE

No, my husband's in his workshop behind the

house. He has a lot to do.

FRANÇOISE

You aren't in need of anything -- I mean as

far as appliances go.

MARIE

No, I've never lacked anything. We've always

had everything we needed for the house.

FRANÇOISE

I'll show you our catalogue. Your home is very pretty. You've arranged it very tastefully.

MARIE

It's just practical, you know.

FRANÇOISE

You don't come from around here.

MARIE

No, we're from Hagondange, in the East. We're retired now, well, I mean, my husband ... We liked this area. Would you like something -- coffee, or tea?

FRANÇOISE

If you don't mind. A cup of tea. Thank you.

MARIE

Make yourself comfortable. I'll make some.

FRANÇOISE

I don't want to take up a lot of your time.

MARIE

No, no, it's a pleasure to see someone. It doesn't happen very often. Since we came here we've hardly seen anyone ... Make yourself at home ... I'll look at your catalogue ... Do you like music? My husband has recorded a lot of good music. Do you like good music? It makes me cry ... Ever since I was a little girl ... I wanted to be an artist. I had a very pretty voice ... I could've succeeded if there'd been anyone to push me, no doubt about it. It's a question of luck ... I still sing, sometimes ... Rarely, since we came here. But I used to have a lot of success at family parties ... Take off your coat ... It'll warm you up, a good cup of tea ... Ceylon ... My husband won't drink anything else. I'll have a cup, too, to keep you company ... Let's see that catalogue.

> (She leafs through the catalogue.)

My, things have changed ... everything changes, don't you think? How old are you, twenty?

FRANÇOISE

Twenty-seven.

MARIE

You look much younger ... I've never looked my
age, either. How old would you say I am?

FRANÇOISE

I don't know ... It's hard to tell ... In your
sixties?

MARIE

I'm seventy-three ... Life has treated me
well. You know, I still turned a few heads in
Hagondange, when I was out shopping ... It's
mainly my figure that's stayed young.

FRANÇOISE

You seem to be in great shape.

MARIE

Oh, much less so, since we moved here. A
little more tea? The inactivity ... the
country ... There's not much to do ... The
garden ... I hardly work in it any more ...
It's too tiring ... and with this weather ...
Do you like music? Would you let me show you
some photos? That would please me. I'll plug
in the fire, too ... It's pretty, isn't it?
My husband's done everything here. He kills

himself with work. He can't sit still -- you know how it is ... Oh, the gondola ... a gift from my daughter ... This is her in this photo. When she was little. She stayed in Hagondange ... This is a painting of my grandson's ... He has a lot of talent. I've got some cookies; would you like some?

FRANÇOISE

Thank you very much, no. I should be on my way. I have other houses to visit. I see that you don't need anything.

MARIE

Yes. Of course. You have other things to do. I understand ... I was so glad to chat with you ... Come and see us again ... I'll consult with my husband ... May I keep the catalogue?

FRANÇOISE

Certainly. Good-bye, Madam, good-bye.

MARIE

I was so happy to spend some time with you;
good-bye, Miss ... Thank you ... thank you
very much.

> (FRANÇOISE exits. MARIE
> closes the door, turns
> off the lights -- the
> gondola, the fire, the
> candlesticks. She turns
> off the music. She sits
> in a chair and weeps.)

> (BLACKOUT)

SCENE TEN

(The bedroom.)

MARIE

Georges -- are you asleep? Georges, answer
me. There's something wrong. You look funny
... Oh, my God!

GEORGES

Don't shout like that. Everything's all
right. Go back to sleep. I'm not sleepy,
that's all ... I'm thinking.

MARIE

You can think without holding the alarm-clock.

GEORGES

I'm telling myself: soon it'll be four
o'clock, in two hours I get up, in two hours I
go to work, as I have for fifty-five years.
Fifty-five years. Fifty-five years of good
and loyal service ... I ask myself if it was
worth it. After all.

MARIE

I never see you any more. You never come out
of your workshop. I'm bored without you,

MARIE (cont.)

Georges. You're not interested in me any more.

GEORGES

I've spent forty-six years of my life with you. I've always loved you; rarely have I thought of any other woman. But now I have to be left alone. Nothing's gone. We have nothing to reproach ourselves for -- a clean life without a blemish. Everything might have been different ... That's the way it is.

MARIE

It's fate.

GEORGES

I don't regret a thing. It's good that you're here, Marie. Sleep. It'll be all right.

MARIE

You work so much you make me worry; you haven't been yourself lately. You wear yourself out, when we could live quietly, enjoy our time some other way.

GEORGES

I have to finish first.

MARIE

Yes, Georges.

(BLACKOUT)

SCENE TEN-A

(The kitchen-dining area. GEORGES and MARIE sitting.)

MARIE

The change of seasons has been sharp this year.

GEORGES

You say that every year.

MARIE

Well, say I repeat myself, but there's a big difference in the temperature between yesterday and today.

GEORGES

Yes ... now we're not going to start discussing the weather.

MARIE

Well, then -- what?

(BLACKOUT)

> (The workshop. GEORGES is
> working. MARIE enters
> with a birthday cake.
> She is singing.)

MARIE

Happy Birthday to you,

Happy Birthday to you,

Happy Birthday, dear Georges,

Happy Birthday to you!

Georges, you've forgotten! Sixty-nine years old today. Make a little space for the cake. The baking-tin was old, so it stuck a little on the bottom ... I hope it's good ... I left out the cream; I know you can't eat it. Everything's fine. I'm happy with you.

GEORGES

It's nice of you, but you shouldn't have wasted money on that ... I'm working ...This place is sacred ... You could've called me ... You never used to come and disturb me at the factory on my birthday ... Leave me alone now. It's very nice of you ... I'll be through at

GEORGES (cont.)

seven ... later ... I'll have some cake ... I
only have five more sheets to do ... I'll come
inside later ... let me finish. Don't be sad
... It's important to me ... Go on, now.

MARIE

Please, I'd like to watch you work. I've
never had a chance to. I'll sit in a corner,
and if you feel like chatting, on a special
day like this -- At least blow out the
candles.

(MARIE sings.)

The Creole girl is dancing,

The boys stand all apart.

They all find her entrancing

But no one knows her heart.

Her little foot moves here --

GEORGES

Stop it! Go away! You don't understand
anything! Work is work, and I've always done
it properly. I won't stop now, just because
I'm retired -- I'm not dead yet .. You all
want to bury me. I'll have gone through it

GEORGES (cont.)

all for nothing. The metal is unwilling, but me, I'll conquer it ... No metal has ever resisted the blow of my hammer ... If I die, it'll be in iron ... Get out!

MARIE

No! I'll stay here. I can't go on ... I'm bored ... I want to see you, to look at you, to talk to you. You can't stop me ... I don't count for you any more -- it's as if I didn't exist ... It's unbearable ... I don't want to see you die in iron ... I want to live peacefully with you, to take the time to live something new. Hagondange is finished ... Do you hear me? FINISHED! You're not in Hagondange any more, there's countryside all around us here ... Come on, let's go for a walk, gather chestnuts ... I don't know what ...

GEORGES

Get out! I can't stop, I can't stop ...

GEORGES (cont.)

> (GEORGES destroys his
> workshop. MARIE exits.
> GEORGES stands alone,
> amidst the wreckage.)

My factory.

> (BLACKOUT)

> (The bedroom. GEORGES is in bed, sick. MARIE is seated on the edge of the bed.)

GEORGES

Don't worry, Marie. I won't leave you just yet -- it's nothing ... Doctors always exaggerate ... Now I'm calm again.

MARIE

That's good, Georges.

GEORGES

That's the way it goes.

> (PAUSE.)

MARIE

Do you feel like some tea?

GEORGES

More like a glass of water.

MARIE

I made a nice vegetable soup for tonight.

GEORGES

You mustn't go to all that trouble.

MARIE

Don't worry about me ... Now, you're going to take care of yourself, promise me that.

GEORGES

It was nerves. That's all ... I'd rather not take these medicines. It's all junk.

MARIE

Do it for me. It's to calm you down.

GEORGES

Yes.

(PAUSE.)

Something snapped inside ... it went off like an explosion ... it's strange ... this is the first time in my life I've had to stay in bed ... Maybe the last.

MARIE

Don't say such things. You scare me.

GEORGES

No, no! I won't leave you ... I told you that -- you can feel these things.

MARIE

Would you like me to put on a little music?

GEORGES

Yes, I really would ... It's been a long time
.. Put on The White Horse Inn ... do you
remember?

MARIE

You had on your best suit, and a beautiful
silk tie. Your shoes were like mirrors.

GEORGES

(Singing.)

I cannot live without your love

Though I'm not worthy of you

I'm reaching for the skies, above

Yet it's true I dare to love you;

I cannot live and still forget you,

I bless the day I met you

And now I pray you may see

You can be life itself to me.

(He laughs.)

MARIE

You sang that all the way home. It was so
funny ... even Papa was charmed.

GEORGES

Those were good times.

>(MARIE plugs in the tape
>recorder, tries a tape at
>various spots.)

MARIE

Now that the weather's turning nice again, I'm
going to start working in the garden. I'll
plant some rosebushes along the fence.

>(The music starts.)

GEORGES

Yes. You could hand me my Digest.

>(MARIE hands him the Rea-
>der's Digest. GEORGES
>turns the pages distrac-
>tedly.)

We could take a trip.

MARIE

Where?

GEORGES

I don't know. We'd have to look into it.
There are so many places to see. Look.

>(He shows her the
>magazine.)

GEORGES (cont.)

Majorca ... One week for 429 francs. Per person. Senior citizens might get reduced rates ... to go away ... I don't know.

MARIE

Georges ... Hagondange ... that's where you'd really like to go, isn't it? Go back to Hagondange. If it's only for a few days, perhaps it wouldn't disturb them ... I'll write to Yvonne.

(BLACKOUT)

SCENE THIRTEEN

                    (MARIE is in the garden,
                    planting rosebushes along
                    the fence. She uses a
                    hoe and a little wooden
                    stick. She is very
                    active. She sings.)

MARIE

Que sera, sera,

Whatever will be, will be,

The future's not ours to see,

Que sera, sera.

What will be, will be.

When I was a little girl,

I asked my mother,

What will I be?

Will I be famous?

Will I be rich?

Here's what she said to me:

<u>MARIE</u> (cont.)

    Que sera, sera,

    Whatever will be, will be,

    The future's not ours to see,

    Que sera, sera.

    .... What ...

Georges!

            (MARIE faints.)

            (BLACKOUT)

> (GEORGES in the kitchen-dining area, wearing a cardigan, writes a letter.)

GEORGES

My little girl,

Following on my telegram, I must confirm this terrible news -- Marie is gone ... It happened yesterday ... I ask myself it it isn't a dream. The burial will take place here next Tuesday, at 9:30 a.m., at St. Joseph's Church ... According to the doctor, she didn't suffer. Everything was going so well, these past few days ... She wore herself out working in the garden -- I told her so, but you know your mother. I don't know what I'm going to do ... certainly sell this house and come back there -- I can't imagine living alone ... It all happened so fast, I'm still unable to think.

I beg you, my little Yvonne, be strong, as I'm trying to be ... It's not easy, I know, but we can't go against Fate. I must ask you, if you

<u>GEORGES</u> (cont.)

will, to tell Aunt Lucienne and the rest of
the family this terrible news, because I
really don't feel able to myself.

There it is ... I'll stop here ... I wait for
you.

Your suffering father,

Georges.

It's a nightmare, Marie.

> (GEORGES gets up, lights
> the log fire, the gon-
> dola, the candlesticks.
> He looks for a tape, puts
> it on the tape recorder.
> After a moment, MARIE's
> voice is heard, singing:)

The Creole girl is dancing

To a tune with a rumba beat;

Her dress flares out, enhancing

The movement of her feet.

Now her body sways with ease,

Like a vine betraying

A breath from a summer breeze.

Her little foot moves here,

Her little foot moves there,

Darting from spot to spot;

A smile to this one here,

A glance to that one there,

Now it's your turn to be caught.

The Creole girl is dancing,

The boys stand all apart;

They all find her entrancing,

But no one knows her heart.

> (The tape plays while
> GEORGES goes to the
> kitchen area and cooks
> two fried eggs for
> himself.)

> (BLACKOUT)

VATER LAND,
THE COUNTRY OF OUR FATHERS
by Jean-Paul Wenzel and Bernard Bloch
Translated from the French by Timothy Johns

CHARACTERS

HERMANN DEUTSCH

SCHULZ

Dead Soldier

WILELM KLUTZ

JEAN

ODETTE

MINA

MONICA

Neighbor

JOANNA

HENRIETTE DUTHEIL

ANNA

HENRI DUTHEIL

FRAU HOLLE

RENE VERNOUX

The same actor can play several parts, for example: Schulz/ Dead Soldier; Odette/Mina; Monica/Neighbor/Joanna; Henriette Dutheil/ Anna.

(WILHELM KLUTZ enters in German uniform.)

WILHELM KLUTZ

I love France, I love the French; but contact with the civilians here is ... well, difficult to say the least. So on free nights, I try to pass myself off as French. I manage to bring this off more and more often now, and whenever a chance encounter gets curious about my accent, I tell him: 'Oh, I come from southern Alsace, had to get out of there -- you know how it is.' I get a lot of pleasure out of this French civilian act. I practice every day, and every day I get a little better. Besides, it's thanks to my knowledge of French that Commander Steiger is ... how shall I say? ... rather partial to me. I do him little favors. 'Tonight, Klutz, is Operation Special Commando. Target: the little ladies. Understand, Klutz? Jawohl, herr Mayor .. Heil Hitler Klutz ...'

(KLUTZ takes off his uni-
form, is now in civvies.)

KLUTZ (cont.)

It was in the course of one of those evening
passes that I met Louis. Louis Dutheil, a guy
about my age, friendly, fun loving, with his
endless supply of jokes and stories, he was a
real ... live-wire, that one. He's only been
in St.-Etienne for two months but he already
knows every little nook and cranny of the
town, and since he comes from the Vosges, his
thick northern accent makes me forget about my
own. Whenever I let slip a German word, he
says, chuckling, 'You Alsatians, you really
are a bunch of Krauts.' His father and
brother have been taken prisoner by the
'boches.' But just as soon as his face starts
to darken, all of a sudden he's bowled over by
some passing girl, and shouts: 'Get a load of
those hams, will ya!' I like Louis; to me
he's the incarnation of France. But apart
from these civilian excursions, I've got to
admit that I'm bored with St.-Etienne. Ever

since the defeat at Stalingrad in February of
'43, troop morale has been at its lowest. All
of us dimly realize that we've lost the war
... I know it must sound shocking, all this
talk about boredom -- especially coming from a
soldier of the Wehrmacht set-up cozily in the
peace and tranquility of occupied France, and
yet ... Scheissdreck ... Afraid of giving
myself away, I see less and less of Louis; his
hatred of Germans has become more and more
open. I no longer go out .. oh yes, once
more, on March 1944, one lovely afternoon in
early Spring.

> (ODETTE GARNIER enters.
> They cross paths, glan-
> cing at one another.)

I forget now if it was before or after the
American bombings in May that I deserted ...
After, right after. Meeting that woman was
decisive. In that room I was renting in
Madame Robert's apartment, all I did was lie
on the bed and think about that woman. A
thousand times, in slow motion, we cross paths

... I can't seem to picture her face, but I
can see again and again her checkered dress,
her shoes, and her raincoat dangling from her
wrist, but her face ... That room is where I
practice my French. On my rare excursions, I
pass by the scene of the encounter, I seem to
see her everywhere, I'm starting to go crazy
... and then, I saw her once more. I followed
her home: avenue Victor Hugo. Odette ...
Odette Garnier. I still didn't dare approach
her; I wasn't ready yet.

ODETTE GARNIER

Back in my room, I'd imitate the Divine
Clara, a fleshy vamp in that private club
Yvonne and her boyfriend Antoine took me to
for my twentieth birthday. During the day, I
work at my father's real estate agency on
St.-Etienne's main street. Home, office, home
... Three times a week I take the mail to the
post-office. Home, office, post-office ... I
always walk very fast, with a cold look in my

70

eyes, to ward off any attempted advances. I
dream of getting away from that interminable
street; I dream, and even my dreams make me
blush. I count my days left as a minor; I'm
bored with St.-Etienne ... There, outside our
windows, is a man pacing back and forth, it's
him I think, that man of March 19th, I turn
out the light to get a better look at him, I
start building an entire fantasy around him,
around us ...

KLUTZ

(Alone)

Why did you have to pass by on just that
night, Louis? You were shouting 'Stop
star-gazing, alsaco, this summer bores me to
tears, let's go get a drink.' You were
talking the usual bull-shit, but this time
with a cynicism that was chilling. Your
father was dead. Your eyes were blazing, spit
drooled from the corners of your mouth. You
dragged me from bar to bar throughout the
night; it was the 24th of June, the festival

of St. Jean, and bonfires everywhere. You
were very loud, much too loud. You'd jump
into the flames: 'It's St. Jean's night, c'mon
and jump you kraut!' Stop it! Right Louis,
I'm not Alsatian, my name is Wilhelm Klutz,
German soldier, I'm a boche, a kraut, a
schleu, a fritz, a maggot. I told him
everything, the whole story. Louis lit into
me. The coals, the smoke, the blood. Louis
with his mouth wide open, and then ...
nothing. Silence. Louis had stopped moving.
I vomited. He was dead. I stared at him and
the longer I stared the more I saw myself --
me, Wilhelm Klutz, dead ... There I was, dead.
Mechanically, with a huge rock, I pounded
Louis' head -- my head -- to a mush. Go get
my uniform, wrapped up in kraft paper back at
Madame Robert's ... run ... run ...
Kriegsengel ... angel of war ... alcoholic
fumes ... undress Louis ... dress Louis up in
my uniform ... military I.D., lighter,
cigarettes ... total silence.

KLUTZ (cont.)

I weep, I weep for the death of Wilhelm Klutz,
German soldier stationed in St.-Etienne. I'm
sober now, my elbow hurts and my nose is
bleeding. As a child my nose used to bleed
after strong emotions. I cover up the body
with rocks, repeating in my head: My name is
Louis Dutheil, I'm a linen-salesman, born in
St. Die in the Vosges. My name is Louis
Dutheil ...

KLUTZ

I'm looking for an apartment.

ODETTE

... For rent or for sale?

KLUTZ

For rent, for rent.

ODETTE

... I'll go ask my father.

(She doesn't move.)

KLUTZ

Miss, allow me to ... My name is Louis Dutheil
... I noticed you in the street and ever since

KLUTZ (cont.)

then ... excuse me for being so frank ... I've been thinking about you ... I can't help it ... I just had to tell you ...

ODETTE

But ... but ...

KLUTZ

Would you have dinner with me tonight? I know it's a bit abrupt, but ....

ODETTE

I don't know, I don't know ... no, not tonight.

KLUTZ

Then when? When?

ODETTE

Tuesday, call me on Tuesday.

KLUTZ

Until Tuesday, then, I don't exist. Until then, my dear Odette.

ODETTE

'Until then, my dear Odette.' 'Otette' he said -- I guess it's his accent. After that memorable Tuesday, after that night in the

74

<u>ODETTE</u> (cont.)

flophouse, everything moved fast. Within the year, I played all the roles up to the hilt: Virgin Daughter, Whore, Wife, Mother. Our son Jean was born in April, St.-Etienne was liberated, Louis became my father's partner, the peaceful days flowed along.

> (A man arrives, HENRI DUTHEIL: short hair, baggy pants, wrinkled jacket, a suitcase and newspaper in his hand.)

<u>HENRI DUTHEIL</u>

I went for a walk down St.-Etienne's main street. Drawn by the smell of fresh-baked bread, I walked into a bakery. Without a ration-ticket I was still able to haggle a small roll, still hot from the oven. Sitting on a bench, I tore open the roll with my thumbs, right under my nose, so I wouldn't lose the smell. I chewed for a long time. I thought back on the prison camp. Allach, buried beneath the snow, roads blocked, the mud, the hatred, the organization, the friendships seized so desperately ... That was

DUTHEIL (cont.)

four months ago, only four months ... 'krieg
vertig.' The German corporal had tears in his
eyes. The Americans. Leclerc himself coming
to shake our hands. The therapy. That trip
across devastated Germany. The lamb we
slaughtered on the side of the road. The
strange taste of freedom. At St.-Die a brass
band was playing the Marseillaise. That was
on the 8th of March, 1945. Peace. Hugs,
songs. St. Die in ruins. Henriette with her
big black eyes. My mother blubbering about
the 'goddamned war, Louis my son, that
goddamned war.' Hero of the Resistance. The
plan to rebuild the city, and that nightmare
about Louis, which finally drove me here ...
His last letter, a postcard dated Christmas
'43, mailed at St.-Etienne ... the ad in the
paper ... Four months.

DUTHEIL

Is this the ... Garnier-Dutheil Agency?

ODETTE

Yes.

DUTHEIL

I'd like to see Monsieur Dutheil.

ODETTE

He isn't here ... can I help you?

DUTHEIL

Well, my name is Henri Dutheil ... and I'm looking for my brother.

ODETTE

You mean Louis!?

DUTHEIL

That's it! Louis ... What a break ... I was just about to leave when I came across your ad in the paper: 'Advice, you say? See Garnier -Dutheil!'

ODETTE

Louis never told me he had a brother ... I'm sorry, let me introduce myself: Odette Dutheil; I'm his wife.

DUTHEIL

Well then ... I guess we're family!

ODETTE

You don't look much like Louis.

DUTHEIL

No doubt I've changed these last four years
... when we were younger, though ... look ...

(He takes out a photo.)

ODETTE

That's not my Louis.

DUTHEIL

But that's my brother ...

ODETTE

That's not Louis!

DUTHEIL

I knew it ... I knew it ... that nightmare ...

PROLOGUE

> (A young man, JEAN, is sit-
> ting against a wall. He
> seems 'out of it'; people
> pass by and stop.)

A LADY

Ought not to stay there, young man, in this
wind you'll catch your death.

JEAN

... the end of the journey ...

1st YOUNG LADY

What's wrong with him?

A MAN

Dead drunk ...

JEAN

... A guy, a fellow, a breeder ...

2nd YOUNG LADY

Don't you have a place to sleep?

1st YOUNG LADY

For three days now he's been hanging around
here.

MAN

He a sailor?

1st YOUNG LADY

I don't think so.

POLICEMAN

All right, the rest of you, move aside ...
you, your papers!

>   (The others leave; JEAN
>   hands over his passport
>   mechanically.)

You French?

JEAN

... with a German father ...

POLICEMAN

What're you doing in Germany?

JEAN

Baden-Baden, Frankfurt, Wuppertal, Hamburg ...

POLICEMAN

>   (Reading from passport.)

Garnier, Jean. Born April the 20th, 1945, in
St.-Etienne, Loire.

JEAN

My Vaterland ... the main entry ... sausage
and beer, beer and sausage ... you see how
skinny I am ... what were you doing during
the war ...

POLICEMAN

Go home, fella.

JEAN

I'd like to be fat .. Understand? Forget it
all in deep fat ... they don't talk about the
war ... American cities ... military convoys,
prisons of silence, three ... third
generation, three months of Germany, three
days, three nights in Hamburg, three days,
three nights not daring to push open the door
to that bistro on Bernhardt noch strasse:
'The Kingfisher'; behind that door, Wilhelm
Klutz, my father ... a paunchy old bar-keeper
... I like your photos better ...

(He looks at a photo.)

HERMANN DEUTSCH

(To JEAN.)

Allemagne Deutschland Germany

Deutschland 82 Das Land unser Vater

Baden Frankfurt Wuppertal St.-Etienne St. Die

    Hamburg Die Juden

Wo sind die Juden Deutschland ohne Juden

Levy Bloch und Blum Blum Blum

Boom Boom

Grosses B kleines Loch

Weiso, wieso kann man Deutschland wieder

    lieben, augucken

And how can we ever love her again,

    face her again, Germany?

Les boches, les fritz, les fridolins, Müller,

    Ivan, Smith and Martin

English zone, eastern zone, pedestrian zone

The feast of ideas, the battle lists of

    ideological banquets

March '82, received injection of nihilism

Rediscover the Black Forest, Pacifismus,

    Neutralismus

Nihilismus ...

Der Deutsche Wald

Röslein, Röslein rot

Röslein auf der heide

SS, SS20, KZ Pershing, your father ...

Dein Vater, wo ist dein Vater

Wo ist Willy

DEUTSCH (cont.)

Du hast Soviel bier und Schnapps getrunken das

    du nicht mehr dein Vater findest

Zuviel Bier und Wurst und Souvlaki Pizza,

    kebab, ketchup, sexshop, Hamburger

Dein Vater, dein Vater ...

Sophienstrasse zweiundachtzig

Baden-Baden, Baden-Baden, 1945.

                    (JEAN, dressed as a German
                    soldier, interrogating
                    KLUTZ.)

JEAN

Name?

KLUTZ

Klutz, Wilhelm.

JEAN

Geboren?

KLUTZ

1920.

JEAN

Geburtsort.

KLUTZ

Erfurt.

JEAN

Color of hair.

KLUTZ

Black.

JEAN

Color of eyes.

KLUTZ

Brown.

JEAN

Mouth.

KLUTZ

Sensual.

JEAN

Family.

KLUTZ

Unstable.

JEAN

Religion.

KLUTZ

...

JEAN

Weight.

KLUTZ

Varies.

JEAN

Profession.

KLUTZ

Prisoner of war.

JEAN

Where?

KLUTZ

France.

JEAN

Member of the Nazi party?

KLUTZ

Nein.

JEAN

Hitler Jugend.

KLUTZ

Ja.

JEAN

Wohim, wofür, wozu, wieso, wieviel, wiewert,
wielange.

KLUTZ

I crossed the border in August of '45. Passed
unnoticed in that mob of poor bastards.
Klutz's driver's license lets me reinvent a
past ... once again. Remnants of Louis
Dutheil still cling to my skin. Odette.
Jean. I have trouble expressing myself in
German. Grandeur and decadence. I left my

86

KLUTZ (cont.)

country in 1942 at the height of her glory,
and now I find her completely stripped,
amnesiac, beggared, scrambling after her
conquerors' cigarette butts. I must have a
thing for occupied countries.

JEAN

Name?

MONICA (1st Young Lady)

Monica Kempf.

JEAN

Geboren.

MONICA

1925.

JEAN

Geburtsort.

MONICA

Augsburg.

KLUTZ

It wasn't until the beginning of winter that I
happened to land in Baden-Baden ... A link
with France ... I moved into the empty

<u>KLUTZ</u> (cont.)

compartment of an abandoned railcar, on a side
track right next to the station ... The
station ... The rumbles, the screams, the hiss
of locomotives and steam.

<u>JEAN</u>

Hitler Youth?

<u>MONICA</u>

Nein.

<u>JEAN</u>

Nazi Party?

<u>MONICA</u>

Nein ... A train-car waiting for an impossible
departure. No need of window-curtains for
privacy; the grease and the soot do the trick.
I have nothing to hide. One night I sleep
with Klutz, the next with Schulz.

<u>JEAN</u>

Name.

<u>SCHULZ</u> (The Man)

Schulz, Herbert.

JEAN

Geboren.

SCHULZ

1905.

JEAN

Beruf.

SCHULZ

Writer ... washed-up writer, a few middling scripts for the UFA and the greater glory of the German forest.

MONICA

When I'm really hungry I sleep with a French soldier or some passing American for a can of corned beef. Klutz, he's the King of Cigarettes. Recycled butts gleaned from the French authorities. Cigarette, corned beef, cigarette for corned beef, a meal-ticket ... Then there's the Red Cross soup; 1600 calories in all on a good day ... no extra effort ... head empty ... the lightbulb overhead never lights up. As for Schulz, he never does a thing. He just stares outside, no, he only

<u>MONICA</u> (cont.)

appears to stare outside ... He's just writing

the same old phrase on the filthy windowpane.

<u>SCHULZ</u>

Und das bedanken wir unseren führer.

And for this we give thanks to the Führer.

<u>JEAN</u>

Hitler Jugend?

<u>SCHULZ</u>

Ja.

<u>JEAN</u>

Member of Nazi party?

<u>SCHULZ</u>

Ja.

<u>JEAN</u>

S.A.?

<u>SCHULZ</u>

Nein ... I always managed to avoid

compromising myself, just a petty Nazi, that's

all ... Four months in Dachau after the

defeat, 'scuse <u>me</u>, the liberation ... the

8th of May, 1945 ... It was on that day that

my wife died in a car accident. Name was

SCHULZ (cont.)

Erna, Erna Filkenstein; she was a Jew ...
after my four months in Dachau, I met Monica
... on the road ... somewhere else ...
Baden-Baden ... then Klutz and the domestic
triangle ... a train-station pot-boiler. The
silence.

JEAN

(Mocking KLUTZ.)

'Odette my love, I'm in Germany. I did
something terrible during the war. I can't
tell you anything now, not yet. But it was
the only way I could meet you. I don't regret
anything. Please come, I can't do without
you. Ask for Wilhelm Klutz, 82
Sophienstrasse, in Baden-Baden. I love you.
Louis. But don't give anyone this address.'

ODETTE

Baden-Baden. The city where this Monsieur
Dutheil works. Why Germany? 'A terrible
thing ... the only way I could meet you ... '

JEAN

Ever since the border, the train makes more
and more stops. Not a smile, not a glance,
you don't speak their language, and you're
afraid.

MONICA

Are you French? Joining your husband? It's
pretty obvious - Soldaten Frau.

ODETTE

And you, you rejoining your family? Or your
boyfriend maybe?

MONICA

I don't have a boyfriend and my parents were
killed in the bombing of Munich ... there's no
family left. I live in Baden-Baden. I ...
manage to get by, if you know what I mean.

FRAU HOLLE (The Lady)

Here in Baden we don't have anything against
the French, madame, but there have been
abuses, too many intolerable abuses. I know,
you're going to tell me that the Germans
didn't exactly treat the French with kid

FRAU HOLLE (cont.)

gloves. But that was war, madame, that was war.

SCHULZ

Ein Reich, ein Volk, ein Führer ... Blöter kuh ...

Forgive them, madame, they know not what they say.

DEUTSCH

Kinda tough to plow your way through, huh Miss? Go ahead 'n step on 'em, they're used to it ... you won't wake 'em up ... Baden-Baden ... best 'o luck, Miss.

SCHULZ

Can I help you with your bag?

ODETTE

No thank you, it isn't very heavy.

FRAU HOLLE

Want some chocolate? I got some chocolate.

ODETTE

No.

MONICA

How 'bout some cigarettes, then? Real
American filter-tips...

> (They try to snatch her
> bag. RENE VERNOUX, an
> official in the French
> military government,
> intervenes.)

RENE VERNOUX

Don't be afraid, madame, they don't mean any
harm; they're just dealing in the black market
like the rest of us back home, it's the only
way they can survive ... You seem a bit lost
... Vernoux, René Vernoux.

ODETTE

I've got to get to ...

JEAN

A friend's.

ODETTE

A friend's place. I'm not too familiar with
the town; he lives on Sophienstrasse.

JEAN

' ... Don't give anyone this address.'

VERNOUX

Sophienstrasse? Not many houses left standing around there. I'll drive you. To your right, there's the new playing field, built for the German youth by the French administration ... To your left, the famous Baden-Baden casino, by some miracle left intact ... Ah, here's number 82. Not much left, but there are curtains up, the mailbox seems new. If you have any problems, don't hestitate to come see me at the central office in Königsallée .. Ask for monsieur Vernoux ... Madame ...

ODETTE

Louis! Louis!

JEAN

René Vernoux ... René Vernoux is a friend of Dutheil's! He's the one who got him to come to Germany to help him reorganize youth services and sports, all within the framework of denazification ... Henri Dutheil is also in Baden-Baden.

DUTHEIL

> (Writing.)

Ever since Henriette's arrival here, morale
has picked up. The apartment used to be so
empty ... Thanks to René Vernoux, my friend
from Allach, I'm getting over the fact that
once again I'm surrounded by Germans. He's a
great help to me in my work.

HENRIETTE

> (Interrupting.)

You know, Henri, about that housekeeper ...
I've been doing some thinking. I really would
prefer not to. I just don't like being served
-- it's embarrassing. And then what would I
do if I didn't have this big apartment to take
care of?

DUTHEIL

' ... The St.-Etienne police still haven't
answered my letter about Louis ... But I
haven't lost hope.'

HENRIETTE

Aren't you going to drink your coffee? This
is the real stuff. I'm starting to learn a
few of the scams around here myself ... By the
way, I've invited the Deniots over for dinner
Tuesday night, so don't get home too late will
you?

DUTHEIL

(Continuing to write.)

' ... With all the German youth groups
dissolved, I'm in charge of organizing a
sports club in Offenburg. I like the work —
you know my passion for sports ... René
thinks that fairly soon we'll have to hand
over the responsibility for the groups to
young Germans. That would allow me to return
to France ... '

HENRIETTE

That way you could keep hunting for your
brother.

DUTHEIL

My brother's dead, I'm almost positive; it's
that guy I want to find.

<u>JEAN</u>

In Sophienstrasse the sun is slowly
disappearing down at the end of the street. A
trolley has forced its way through the rubble,
pushing rocks to the side, rocks which women
tirelessly hand to each other in a methodical
rhythm ... There's no one home at 82. You
wait. From time to time you hear the creak of
a cart, a pushcart on the pavement, loaded
with furniture ... it's the twilight hour, the
transitition from day to night, oppressive.

<u>ODETTE</u>

Some music ...

<u>JEAN</u>

From a hurdy-gurdy. You get up, move timidly
a little closer, afraid of getting lost.

<u>ODETTE</u>

A travelling carnival ...

<u>JEAN</u>

In a deserted lot, the smell of beignets, a
merry-go-round with wooden horses, too small.
Soldiers with their families. A raffle.
Multi-colored dolls. And there in the middle,
the old man surrounded by children is cranking
his hurdy-gurdy ... You move closer.

> (DEUTSCH sings Goethe's Erlkönig.)

ODETTE

> (Sings softly.)

'Petite fille purdue

à la recherche de mon amour

en pays inconnu ...'

JEAN

You've already forgotten your reason for being

here ... The carnival no longer exists. Only

the night, and the silence.

> (ODETTE panics.)

ODETTE

Sir ... Do you know of a hotel or a place to

sleep?

> (She gestures wildly, try-
> ing to communicate.)

DEUTSCH

Schlafen? Cigarettes?

ODETTE

I don't smoke.

DEUTSCH

Geld, Geld, pulver, money.

>   (ODETTE pulls a bill out
>   of her pocket.)

ODETTE

French money.

DEUTSCH

Gut geld Gut Kammen Kammen! ... Schlafen oder

bumsen ...

>   (They arrive in front of a
>   blockhouse.)

... hier schlafen.

ODETTE

But ... This is a blockhouse!

DEUTSCH

Ja, ja, gut blockhouse schlafen.

FRAU HOLLE

Don't be afraid, miss, schlafen, schlafen. I

got two legs, miss, one Aryan, the other, non.

At night, I unscrew the non-Aryan, and hang

it up on the wall ... There's no more

electricity on Nietzsche Street, and sometimes, in the flickering candle-light, I raise my eyes without meaning to and see my leg moving up there, my wooden leg dancing and twisting on the wall ... My name's Lotte Holle. I'm an Aryan woman, with two legs during the day, and only one at night. I can understand a non-Aryan leg with a body that moves and dances and twists around on the wall when the candle flickers. But that it also has a face, a face that can scream and laugh and mock me like it mocked me back in '43 when we lost Stalingrad, I just can't understand that ... no, really can't understand ...

> (Elsewhere, RENE VERNOUX and DUTHEIL are watching a soccer game.)

DUTHEIL

I've got to admire your calm, René ... What with the American breakfasts, the Russian zakouskis and the English teas, it's impossible to get a simple proposal through.

VERNOUX

I'm just stubborn ... I'll manage to make them understand ... Germany really is paying off her debt.

DUTHEIL

You see that goalie over there? That's Herbert Schmidt, guy I was telling you about. Pretty soon I think he'll be able to take over for me.

VERNOUX

It's a good thing you are here, Henri ... Hey, what's wrong? Henri? ...

DUTHEIL

That guy who just passed by. I think he's ... he's skinnier, features are sharper, but ... I can't believe this ...

JEAN

(To ODETTE.)

Still nobody there at 82. Still the sun hasn't come up, but men and women are already in the rubble handing each other rocks. You're worn out. You don't know what to do ..

JEAN (cont.)

reluctantly, you decide to go back to
St.-Etienne.

ODETTE

But ...

JEAN

You go back to St.-Etienne.

> (She starts on her way
> and bumps into HENRI
> DUTHEIL.)

ODETTE

You!

DUTHEIL

You're here because of him, aren't you?

ODETTE

Who else?

DUTHEIL

I might've known ... You know where he is,
don't you?

ODETTE

Leave me alone!

DUTHEIL

There's no use lying, because I've seen him.
He got away this time, but I'll find him

DUTHEIL (cont.)

again. I also know that your husband's name
is Wilhelm Klutz. He was just about to land a
job as an interpreter with the French. He was
a German soldier stationed in St.-Etienne from
'43 to '45.

ODETTE

You're lying!

DUTHEIL

He murdered my brother on June 24, 1944.

ODETTE

You're lying! Louis's no murderer.

DUTHEIL

Listen to me, Odette.

ODETTE

Louis is not a murderer.

DUTHEIL

His name is Wilhelm Klutz. He's a German.
You've been deceived. The marriage doesn't
count ... just give me his address ...

> (ODETTE runs away and
> throws herself into the
> arms of JEAN. They em-
> brace.)

JEAN

My father ... where is my father ...

KLUTZ

No, I'm not in the country on some dirt road winding around a hlll; not some explorer discovering an ancient city buried deep in the heart of a virgin forest. No. I'm in Frankfurt. Beneath my feet, part of the ruins of Frankfurt are piled high in dirt-covered mounds. Weeds, moss, and scrub brush have swallowed up Frankfurt. And then this silence ... So where are the human beings? Laid out down below, no doubt. Silence, and the twitter of mockingbirds. Lying down on top of the city, for a long time I look up at the heavens, and the heavens remain silent. Their silence no longer frightens me. I'm at peace, my mistake is buried underneath, the grass has grown back over, and the heavens do not judge me. If I weren't so hungry I think I could almost fall asleep here, and sleep for a long, long time.

(KLUTZ falls alseep at the
foot of the wall.
DUTHEIL enters, inter-
rupting two lovers.)

DUTHEIL

Oh excuse me ... I didn't think anyone was

here ... I would like to speak to Wilhelm

Klutz.

SCHULZ

He left.

DUTHEIL

Baden-Baden?

SCHULZ

Look, I'm not the guy's nursemaid.

DUTHEIL

You his friend?

SCHULZ

Could be ... Don't be so nosy, huh? I'm

clean.

DUTHEIL

Aren't you bothered at all by this stench?

SCHULZ

Why don't you go get fucked, you goddamn ...

DUTHEIL

Watch your language ... I'd hate to have to haul you in.

SCHULZ

Good idea. At least then I'd have something to eat. You fucking French, you're the worst ... revanchists ... You didn't win the war ... If it hadn't been for your Allies every last one of you would be Nazis ... all united against Bolshevism ... Schiesfranzose.

MONICA

Halt's maul, Herbert.

DUTHEIL

She's right. Just tell me where Klutz is.

SCHULZ

You can fucking go to the devil.

DUTHEIL

Great ... Have a nice day - both of you.

JEAN

Klutz, Dutheil, Dutheil, Klutz. I follow you, you follow me. What the fuck am I doing here? ... Check the phone-book. Klutz A., Klutz B., Klutz Dieter, Klutz U., Klutz V., Klutz

JEAN (cont.)

Werner ... Germany's rotting my brain ...
always raining ... the trams, the wires in the
sky ... Baden ... Frankfurt and St.-Etienne
... all these towns look alike. Sachsenhausen
... Startbahnwest ... America mired down in
the ditch of defeat ... a decor ... Frankfurt
... the post-war decor ... Frankfurt 1946.

>   (DEUTSCH, FRAU HOLLE, and
>   FRANTZ the musician
>   enter. They surround
>   KLUTZ, collapsed against
>   a wall.)

DEUTSCH

Hemde, Mantel, strümpfe, Amerikanische strümpfe. Nylon stockings direkt aus Amerika. 5 marks mann, 5 marks nylon stockings.

FRAU HOLLE

Ought not to stay there, young man, you'll catch your death.

KLUTZ

... Death?

FRANTZ

It's been sung to death already: 'Enjoy the war, for the peace will be pitiless.'

FRAU HOLLE

>   (Sings, clearly impro-
>   vising)

In Frankfurt, when the night time falls,

Like the bombs that fell the other day,

There's always a way to tie one on.

> (DEUTSCH hands her a
> bottle of booze ... but
> it's empty.)

In Frankfurt now, when all is dark,

And not a drop is left to suck,

We jig a tour around this wreck,

And if we trip a mine, don't give a fuck!

> (FRAU HOLLE and DEUTSCH
> execute a funny dance,
> wooden leg and man-
> nequin's leg.)

In Frankfurt, when the sun has set,

You might imagine nothing's left,

And yet you almost always find,

A little love that's left behind.

> (ANNA'S voice is heard.)

ANNA (Second Young Lady)

'I am called Victory here,

And War was my father,

Peace is my daughter dear —

Already looks like my father.'

ANNA (cont.)

>   (ANNA appears, exchanges
>   glances with KLUTZ.)

Come on.

KLUTZ

I don't have much to offer you.

ANNA

That'll do, come on.

JEAN

TB, TB, syphillis, syphillis, TB!

KLUTZ

What've I got to lose?

JEAN

Your balls!

>   (ANNA and KLUTZ walk side
>   by side.)

KLUTZ

Those flashes over there ... what is that?

ANNA

Soldering irons. They're fixing the bridges
over the Main.

KLUTZ

Electric night ...

ANNA

You in hiding?

KLUTZ

Not any more.

ANNA

Here it is, right here.

KLUTZ

It's as deep as hell itself ... Kinda like a
boat.

ANNA

Yeah, for a ride down the gutter ... the rats
here have become my brothers ... Here! This
is my day for good deeds.

> (She hands him a ciga-
> rette.)

KLUTZ

I'm not asking for anything.

> (Silence. ANNA sings
> softly the König in
> Thule of Goethe. They
> smoke.)

ANNA

To America!

KLUTZ

To America.

> (They embrace passion-
> ately. JEAN can't stand
> the situation, and inter-
> venes.)

JEAN

Dutheil moved on to Frankfurt just after the interview with Schulz and Monica ... he went to Frankfurt because ... just as he's leaving the one remaining room left intact at number 82, his eyes are drawn to a poster stuck to the door. It shows a satyr standing in the middle of a bright green ticket. Across the top is written 'Frankfurt, July 10' ... you remember ... Schulz sends him to the devil and the next second he finds himself face to face with one in a thicket ... Dutheil likes these coincidences. He leaves for Frankfurt ... in the American zone ... he arrives in Frankfurt ... at the train-station ... right next to the train-station.

> (DUTHEIL, SCHULZ, FRAU
> HOLLE, MONICA, A G.I.,
> DEUTSCH, MINA.)

G.I.

Come on!

MONICA

Nein.

G.I.

Come on, goddammit.

MONICA

Nein.

G.I.

You fuckin' German ... what the hell do you
want?

MONICA

Nothing!

G.I.

Chocolate?

MONICA

Nein!

G.I.

Cigarette?

MONICA

I do not smoke and I hate chocolate.

G.I.

You fuckin' German ...

>   (He   throws   down   his
>   cigarette   in   disgust;
>   three people scramble for
>   it; DEUTSCH comes up with
>   it.)

114

DEUTSCH

Lucky Strike, Lucky Strike, who wants a Lucky
Strike? Five marks, five marks, direkt aus
Amerika.

> (He lights the cigarette,
> laughs, and starts to
> sing softly 'Deutschland,
> über alles.' Little by
> little, all the others
> join in except for MINA
> and DUTHEIL. Laughter.
> The song is contagious,
> even the G.I. sings a-
> long, and dies laughing
> at 'in der Welt.' He
> gets a round of applause.
> All exit, except MINA and
> DUTHEIL.)

MINA

Amazing, huh? ... Are you French?

DUTHEIL

Yeah.

MINA

... Voltaire, Rousseau, Leon Blum, Paris ...
La liberté.

DUTHEIL

You're not German? Your accent seems ...

MINA

No. I was born in Vilno in Poland. And then
...

DUTHEIL

And then?

MINA

... Laubwalde in Thuringen ... it was just a
tiny little prison camp ...

DUTHEIL

I'm very sorry.

MINA

For what? You know, if I hadn't been a Jew,
who knows? Maybe I too would've been ... does
that shock you?

                    (ANNA and KLUTZ opposite.)

ANNA

Is that the one?

KLUTZ

Yes.

ANNA

Why don't you go see him?

KLUTZ

Not just yet ...

ANNA

Let's go to Wuppertal, to my parents, we'll be
better off there.

KLUTZ

I've had it with this cat and mouse game.

ANNA

You go on ahead ... I'll join you as soon as
possible ... two or three days at the most.

KLUTZ

Anna ...

ANNA

Go on ...

DUTHEIL

What the fuck am I doing here? Just what the
fuck ... ? Sitting on this rock, on top of
thousands of dead people, surrounded by gray
weeds and twisted metal and boulders blown to
bits. 'You didn't win the war.' 'Germany
really is paying off her debt.' I give up. I
belong in St. Die ... with Henriette, not in

DUTHEIL (cont.)

this desert of ruins, gnawed by memories of
the dead. I give up ... Go to the devil,
Klutz, go to the devil ... Tomorrow I'm going
to go back to Baden, hand in my resignation,
and go back home ... go back home ...

ANNA

(To DUTHEIL.)

Monsieur! Monsieur! Wilhelm Klutz is in
Wuppertal, in the Ruhr District.

JEAN

Wuppertal. Overhead metro, broken beer-
bottles, greasy paper. Wuppertal ...
basically its dirty. The punks scream and
snicker. Sie grinsen, sie grinsen ...

(FRAU HOLLE and FRANTZ
extend this vision of
JEAN'S.)

FRAU HOLLE

Sie grinsen, sie grinsen

Wuppertal, Wuppertal, hard Wuppertal

Wuppertal, Wuppertal no smiles at all

The long street, street too long

Fix on the photo the marks of the past

Bursts of acid, clouds of steel

Sulphuric, sulphurous Rita Pausch Punki

   Ritsch

Wuppertal, Wuppertal, hard Wuppertal

Wuppertal, Wuppertal no looks at all.

I buy a pipe a pear a peach expresso

Willy where's Willy my father where's

   father

Polite placidity of prudent youth.

A little town in California in the sunny

   month of May

Wuppertal, Wuppertal, hard Wuppertal

Wuppertal, Wuppertal no future at all

Mad with lust for food

I stuff myself with shit at Schnellimbiss

Crammed fat, cadaver sauteed

You as well my father

You were a Viking

Pride indifference I don't exist,

   I'm merely wind

Wuppertal, Wuppertal, hard Wuppertal

Wuppertal, Wuppertal no smiles at all

All you did was pass away, pass away

Above all no smiles Willy

Above all no smiles

The long street, street too long

Fix on the photo the marks of the future

Wuppertal ...

Wuppertal ... no looks at all.

A little town in Texas in the sunny month

   of May

The D.J. explodes on his needle

Great sound top level play it again Sam

Wuppertal town without looks

Wuppertal town without smiles

Wuppertal Wuppertal hard Wuppertal

Wuppertal Wuppertal no smiles at all

Wuppertal Wuppertal no looks at all

Wuppertal Wuppertal no future at all

Wuppertal it's you I love

WUPPERTAL 1947

(A man addresses KLUTZ.)

DEAD SOLDIER

Do you see me, sir? I do exist, don't I? You
see sir, it's just that ever since yesterday,
I've had my doubts ... for two years I was a
prisoner in Russia, in Siberia for two years,
sir ... Or else I am in fact dead and you are
too, that's a possibility one shouldn't
reject, since you see, sir, you are the first
person in the last two days who has seen me
... It's up to you, sir ... Am I dead? My
wife, is she a liar? I know you must have
some idea, some answer, I know. I'm a POW
who's come home. While I'm walking through
the city, the barber doesn't answer my
greeting, then the baker, then my neighbor;
lots of people I used to know ... they don't
answer me ... I say hello Hans ... Hello
Madame Schlid, hello Herbert, and every time
they just turn away with a blank face, and

they never answer, they pretend they don't see
me ... at first I said to myself, god how you
must've changed, George my boy, nobody
recognizes you any more ... and I started to
laugh ... Hey! ... Wolfgang, the street-
sweeper, can't you recognize a friend any
more? He turns around but I can tell he's
looking right past me, casually turns back
around and keeps on sweeping the street ...
god knows what I must look like, to be so
totally unrecognizable ... how long has it
been since you looked in the mirror, George my
boy? Ah, it doesn't matter, my wife will be
the most beautiful mirror of all. The house
where I live is still standing. I climb the
stairs. My neighbor across the hall, old
Busch, is coming down with his dog in his
arms. Busch, that old rascal, he's survived
it all. He bumps into me without even
apologizing. 'There's another one who just
passes right through you,' I say to myself. I
knock on the door ... Helga! I cry; Helga,

it's me! ... for a long time I wait there at the door. Helga! Open up, it's me, George. Your husband's come home ... then the door opens and a black guy appears. 'Fuck off, will ya? They ain't no Helga here.' But over his shoulder I see her standing there like a statue, chewing on her handkerchief. I hold out my hand to her. The black guy shoves me back and says: 'You're dead, bro' ... dead. So don't gimme any fuckin' shit.' His German wasn't the best. 'Helga, tell him, will you?' She doesn't move, still chewing on her handkerchief. 'Go to the cemetery, bro', ain't no mo' room for you here,' and he slams the door ... that black guy, he's the only one who saw me, but if I'm dead, I say to myself, then surely he's the devil ... I walked across the city to the cemetery, and then I understood. I saw the tombtone, and read: George Heckel, born April 9, 1920 ...

                    (KLUTZ knocks on the
                    door.)

NEIGHBOR

You come for the apartment?

KLUTZ

... Uh, no, I've come to see Mr. and Mrs.
Fischer. Their daughter Anna sent me.

NEIGHBOR

You gotta be kiddin' me. Been two weeks since
they left us.

KLUTZ

Where to?

NEIGHBOR

Where to? Goddam cemetery that's where. I
mean I can't tell ya exactly where, but ...

KLUTZ

You mean, they're ...

NEIGHBOR

Yep. Reformed 'emselves with gas. Mr.
Fischer he wasn't doin' so hot those last few
days, guess you'd hafta say his conscience was

days, guess you'd hafta say his conscience was
buggin' him. The English they figgered out
what he was up to durin' the war ... and he
was s'posed to have to pay for it. Guess he
preferred to de-nazify his own self ... all
alone ... well, that is, with his wife ...
gassed 'emselves ... stuck their heads right
into the oven ... It's like my husband said:
'With all that gas they used we coulda cooked
a whole month' ... but who are you, anyway?

KLUTZ

Oh ... nobody.

DEUTSCH

Tattoo anybody? Anybody for a tattoo proves
you were interned by the Nazis? Certificate
and all, all correct and proper, 100 marks for
the tattoo with the certificate ... for only
100 marks, your worries are over.

JEAN

(To KLUTZ.)

Endless suburbs, the sprawling outskirts along
the Wupper ... brick houses with adjoining

JEAN (cont.)

patches of lawn ... little brick houses all
alike, huddled together as if to protect
themselves from bombs ... Smokestacks, mine-
shafts, factories shut down, abandoned,
dismantled, and ...how shall I say? ...
disaffected ... Krupp, Opel ... wide avenues,
trams, the sky latticed with wires ... the
city is long, so long ... and very far away, a
procession ... with music ... it's the
carnival ... the Carnival of Wuppertal.

            (A group arrives wearing
            identical masks: FRAU
            HOLLE, the NEIGHBOR, the
            DEAD SOLDIER, MINA,
            DEUTSCH.)

FRAU HOLLE

Don't just sit there like a statue, come on!

WOMAN

Join up, you traitor!

DEAD SOLDIER

Hey Willy! Can't recognize a friend any more?

ANNA

C'mon! C'mon! It's high time, Willy.

>   (KLUTZ hesitates, looks at
>   Jean, then decides to
>   join in the Carnival. He
>   dons the same mask as the
>   others.)

JEAN

It was at that very moment that you forgot
about us, that you forgot about me .. at that
very moment ...

KLUTZ

Scheise!!

JEAN

>   (Shouting.)

Dutheil! Dutheil! Look how happy they are,
how much they're enjoying themselves ... for
fourteen years they've kept their mouths shut.

DUTHEIL

>   (Screaming.)

Klutz! Klutz! Show yourself! Show yourself,
Klutz! Klutz!

>   (He plunges into the pro-
>   cession; they grab him,
>   manhandle him, and leave
>   him unconscious at the
>   foot of the wall.)

DEAD SOLDIER

He's dead drunk.

FRAU HOLLE

We ought to carry him out of here, before he

gets himself trampled to death.

NEIGHBOR

He's French, a party-pooper ... Easy, easy,

put him down on that slab. You hear me,

Monsieur Dutheil? You hear me? He can't hear

me.

ANNA

Easy now ... Be careful, all of you.

KLUTZ

Give him some air, he needs air ... don't give

up yet, my brother, the end of the road is in

Hamburg. In Hamburg.

JEAN

> (To   DUTHEIL,   still
> unconscious.)

Winsen, Hoopte, Rosenwide, Bullen. You follow
the railroad track, the distant glimmer of
Hamburg nibbles away at the night and swallows
up the moon ... A level crossing ... a square
of light ... the yapping of a dog ... laundry
hung up in a yard ... the suburbs. And now
the entire sky is a grayish yellow. You're
unaware of any fatigue. You plunge deeper
into Hamburg. No, it isn't that you penetrate
deeper into the city, it's that the city which
little by little encloses you ...

DEUTSCH

> Heimat, eine sterne
>
> Unser Himmel leuchtet
>
> Wie ein Diamant
>
> Tansend Sternen
>
> Stehen in weiter ferne
>
> Auch dich ein mal möcht' ich

DEUTSCH (cont.)

    Wieder sehen

    Schöne, abend Stunde

    Unser Himmel leuchtet

    Wie ein Diamant

    Tausend Sternen

    Stehen in weiter ferne

    Schicken viele grüsse aus dem

    (Heimat land - Vater land)

    Heimat, O Heimat

    Ich mocht dich einmal wieder

    sehen

    (twice)

Ain't hot today is it?

DUTHEIL

That light down there ... what is that?

DEUTSCH

Hamburg, Hamburg starting to light itself up
again.

DUTHEIL

... Hamburg ..

DEUTSCH

A word of advice, young fella. Turn right
around while there's still time. Hamburg is a
man-eater, she's gobbled up a million of 'em
in two nights -- one less wouldn't matter
much.

(He goes away singing.)

DUTHEIL

Hamburg, the end of the road. Unless you
plunge into the sea ...

JEAN

Walk! C'mon and walk, my brother.

(He laughs hysterically.)

ANNA

Klutz is sitting on the edge of the boardwalk,
his head thrown back, his eyes half-closed.
The ocean breeze caresses his face, and a
faint smile plays on his lips ... He doesn't
move, but his eyes are following the flight of
a sea-gull in the dark sky over Hamburg. The
din from the port, the blasts from the

fog-horns, the shouts of the dockers -- none of this bothers him. His war has come to an end here, in Hamburg.

KLUTZ

Behind me the city is ready for reconstruction, impeccable in its ruin. Already new houses are springing up around Alster Lake. I'm waiting for Anna, the wind in my nostrils ... A seagull dives into the oily waters of the port: the Elbe. From here I can see the astonished eye of the fish, the blood-filled gills gaping wide ... the pride of the seagull? Bewitched by Hamburg, the dark sky, the breeze, the groan of the boats leaving Hamburg ... Am I really thinking of getting away from Germany? Bewitched by Anna, by her voice, her unexpected love. She didn't allow herself a single tear over her parents' death. 'I'm supposed to have a cousin in Hamburg, let's give that a try.' And that was all.

(ANNA   steadily   ap-
                            proaches.)

ANNA

He sits up, stares a long time out over the
water, scrapes together a little pile of
pebbles to throw into the Elbe. Gravel, the
busted rubble and the dust of bombs ... the
smell of rubber, of paint, of fish, of oil ...
the ripple of the waves ... And now, with a
piece of chalky rock, he draws something on
the greasy pavement ... no, he's writing
something.

                    (She's beside him now; He
                    hasn't seen her.)

'Dutheil, here I am; and here I'll be
forever.'

                    (KLUTZ tries to erase the
                    writing, ANNA prevents
                    him. She coughs.)

ANNA

No, leave it!

KLUTZ

This Hamburg air isn't doing you any good.

ANNA

Well, that's it ... Rudolph has agreed.

KLUTZ

How'd you manage that?

ANNA

One guess.

> (Silence.)

> (Laughingly.)

At first he got on his high horse about it.
You know how he is ... 'Willy has no right to
talk to me like that, I'm the boss around
here.' 'Okay, Rudy, okay. Have it your way,
just go on living in your filthy little cafe.'
'No but really now Anna. I took the both of
you in without a penny ... I put you up, feed
you ... though god knows I don't have much
myself.' ... 'Who's denying that, Rudy?
Willy's quite an operator, you know, right now
it can all be earned down at the docks, this
city's bristling with activity' ... And then I
showed him the floor-plan. 'If you cannot see

ANNA (cont.)

that a hotel-restaurant two steps from the
port on Bernhardt noch strasse is an absolute
gold mine, then my poor Rudy you are a
hopeless moron' ... 'Well, after all, if it's
not gonna cost me anything ... but listen,
with my ass hocked up to the hilt, I'm not
gonna be able to help' ... it's working,
Willy, it's working.

KLUTZ

And then I suppose it was later that you ...

ANNA

Come on!

JEAN

It's daybreak. The sounds of morning: cars,
trucks, pedestrians, all the bustle of any
normal morning. The smell of frying onions,
of fish ... Dutheil near the port. Why isn't
he hurrying?

DUTHEIL

A big bowl of coffee, please, and a great big
plate of your hash!

JOANNA

There sir, there you are ...

That man ... I can't figure out who he could be ... Sure isn't a German, not with that accent ... A sailor, maybe? ... No, don't think so. With the occupying forces: No way, look at his wrinkled clothes and that three days' growth ... Unemployed? ... Could be ... Something's happened to him ... something serious ... he looks so far away ... looks right past people ... Doesn't seem either sad or broken, though ... Ah, he's French ... that way he has of sopping his plate with a piece of bread ... What's he doing here in Hamburg?

DUTHEIL

Another coffee, please.

JOANNA

This one's on me ... It really is a pleasure to see you eat.

JEAN

Every day Henri comes back to the diner to eat ... All day long he wanders around Hamburg,

JEAN (cont.)

around the docks ... no longer looking for Wilhelm Klutz, no longer looking for anything ... He has no desire to go back home ... he's stopped writing anyone ... he never thinks back on the past. Sometimes he utters certain strange phrases ...

DUTHEIL

Hamburg has me bewitched ... We eating together tonight?

JOANNA

I know.

(Laughter.)

EPILOGUE

(JEAN at the foot of the
wall.   People   pass,
stop.)

JEAN

Baden, Frankfurt, Wuppertal, Hamburg ... three

days, three nights wandering around Hamburg,

unable to bring myself to walk into this

bistro on Bernhardt noch strasse ... "The

Kingfisher" ... No, not fear ... three days,

three nights ... beer ... beer ... beer ...

St.-Pauli ... live-show ... peep show ... hard

core ... topless ... the port ... supertankers

... freighters ... Japanese ... gigantic

shipyards ... the ocean breeze ... Wilhelm

Klutz   ...   put   off   that   encounter   ...

ridiculous ... so this is where you live,

Willy, so this is where you live, my father

... live show, peep show, hard core, topless,

stop, it's too much ... stop ... A guy ... a

fellow ... an absence ...

                    (KLUTZ appears at the
                    door.)

KLUTZ

What is it?

JEAN

Mister Wilhelm Klutz? ... My name is Jean ...
Jean Garnier.

KLUTZ

I don't believe you ... where were you born?

JEAN

St.-Etienne, the 20th of April, 1945.

KLUTZ

Mother's first name?

JEAN

... Odette ... Odette Garnier.

KLUTZ

Grandparents?

JEAN

... Charles and Marie Garnier. Real estate
agency on Rue Gambetta in St.-Etienne ...
Would you by chance like to see my papers?

KLUTZ

Yes ... for sure. Your passport, please.

(Short pause.)

Come in ... if you aren't Jean ... I'll kill
you.

Introduction

I was born in Tulsa, Oklahoma, a town where I grew up loving books and writing. I have written poetry for most of my life. This book is an extension of my hard work and dedication.

I went to Carver Middle School and Booker T. Washington High School, two of the best schools in the country. I have performed poetry in spoken word form, but I have always wanted to be a published author.

I first got my start as a published author in the fall of 2013, when I was selected among others to have one of my poems published in an anthology of poetry. Again, in the fall and spring of 2014, I was selected to be in another anthology of poetry. Even though I was published, I wanted my own book, and now I have my chance.

This book is for my family and friends who helped me live so that I may break the chains that binded me. To my mother and father, Charisma and Earl Alston, who taught me to live life with elegance. To my sisters, Alexis and LaShaelyn, who pushed me all the way. To my brothers, Terrell and Malachi, who always had a joke to tell. To my grandparents, aunt, and uncle, who prayed and gave me their blessings. Thank you for everything.

Charity Crawford aka Poetic Melodies

Poetic Inspiration

"The way to inspiration is found in the most unusual places. The unknown is familiar only in silence, and that's where you find your inspiration. Because poetry and the unknown are one and the same." - Poetic Melodies

Funny Limericks

There was a man named Steve,

On his head a talking weave,

It started to cough,

Then it fell off,

That time he was naïve.

There was a man named Lang,

Whose mustache went "Bang!"

Everywhere he goes,

People laughed at his nose,

Plus everyday he sang.

Inspires

How can we inspire? It takes a lot of dedication.

To teach them not to fear. To live life with elation.

What do we, as individuals, need to reach our

destinations?

Individuals

Need

Special

People

In

Real

Everyday

Situations

Try Me

In life, I can make it

In heart, I can take it

My soul, can't be broken

My mind, not a token

So you think, that you have me

But you, can't even touch me

So try, as you might

But what you find, will be a sight

Bring It On

Blood, sweat, and tears

Pain, perspiration

Bone breaking fears

No expiration

Life giving strength

It's almost done

But I can keep on going

Bring it on

Poetic Torture

"Our minds is where we feel the most pain. Where we have the most questions, and so, is the root of our torture. And it never ends until we put it on the paper, and then speak it out loud." - Poetic Melodies

Doubt

Captivity,

Shame,

Thinking you have nothing to gain,

What's left for you?

You're feeling the pressure times two,

A slave to your mind,

What are you trying to find?

The hallway gets longer,

You want to feel stronger,

Here you are.

Choking,

It seems too far,

Smoking,

Nothing but doubt,

That becomes your name,

What is life about?

It's the end of the game,

No one can save you,

You're all alone,

Falling in the shadows,

Doubting,

Fall flat on your face,

It's the end of the race,

Still doubting?

No, it's done.

Maybe

Maybe, a word to say what can or cannot be.

Maybe, a word that might define your destiny.

Maybe it is, maybe it isn't, who can tell the difference?

Maybe I will fall in love.

Maybe I'll get hurt.

Maybe I will lose my wings.

Maybe I'll never be able to sing.

Maybe the birds will never fly again.

Maybe someday I'll have a friend.

Maybe this day my dreams will come true.

Maybe this day hell might come over you.

Maybe we'll live in an endless nightmare.

Maybe this day we'll choose to dare.

Maybe I will get lost in my addiction.

Maybe I will be able to tell fact from fiction.

Maybe once I was bound in chains.

Now maybe I can learn to be free again.

Maybe now I can have some joy.

Maybe now I can find my peace.

Maybe my dreams will have endless fame.

And maybe now I will remember my name.

Questions

Maybe, just maybe...

Love overcomes all situations...or so they say

Can we really make a difference among our generation?

Are you sure that you know what you know?

Do you think that maybe it was you? Or me?

Or someone that was kin to thee?

Invisibility is a drug that is addicting,

Some may overdose on this drug,

Invisible, ignored, there are so many more...

Search your mind. Seek your heart.

Lift your spirit to the heavens.

Breathe deeply,

Let the calmness flow,

Steady your mind on where to go.

What can be done about the way that we feel?

Whether it is fake or whether it is real?

I wish that sometimes I was never here.

Since everyone thinks that I have certain fears.

But since I'm living in this nightmare of a life...

I will try to live it as my best.

Maybe, one day, in another life

I don't understand

I don't understand

How we can even say that we're equal

Why is the truth the only thing that doesn't get a sequel

I don't understand

How we can live like stone walls

Never showing a crack of feeling

I don't understand

Why do we have to prove that we're authentic

Just to be another statistic in society's lies

I don't understand

How we can let the world go by

Without us there to guide it

I don't understand

If justice and liberty really carry their name

Then why do we have to be insane

Just to be "accepted"

I don't understand

How we can sleep at night

Knowing the lies we tell our children

Spreading our own fears and prejudices

For our own private healing

I don't understand

Why do we use religion as an excuse

To try and shield ourselves

I don't understand

How we can bind others to laws

Like we binded our brothers and sisters in chains

I don't understand

If we can do better than the average of ourselves

Then why don't we

I don't understand

How we can deprive others of living

Yet tell ourselves to live life to the fullest

I don't understand

How we can live, walk, and talk

Like there is nothing wrong

You're weak when you're supposed to be strong

I try to understand but I can't

Remember the advantages we used to take

Remember the relationships we used to create

Remember the risks we used to take

Remember the love we used to make

I don't understand

What happened

You can fly higher than the trees

Be all that you can be

What's holding you back

In the shadows

You don't understand

But neither do I

People

Have you ever wondered why we are the way that we are?

Did it ever occur to you that we are each special?

God's workmanship...

Have you ever tried,

To think of yourself as a knot untied?

Some of us are just waiting for that sweet chariot to take us

for a ride.

Our Lord will come like a thief in the night,

Only He knows when the time is right.

Good or bad,

High or low,

There we will go with our hearts in tow.

So if you are wondering,

Just take it from me.

This is why God created the people's diversity.

Diversity

Diversity is walking into a restaurant without being served poorly.

Black, white, Hispanic, Native American,

all these don't matter as long as you know there is peace.

Long time ago when it was a shame to be black,

They used us in slavery and made us live in shacks.

What is diversity?

Well, I'll tell you, so you'll see.

Diversity is you being you, and me being me.

Living this world in perfect harmony.

With the world hating all kinds of cultures.

Didn't Jesus say to love one another?

Diversity means love, trust, and faith in another.

For a neighbor, stranger, sister, and brother.

Can you diversify a slave and his master?

From what happened before will become it's after.

God made us all to live in peace, not apart because the

hate won't cease.

Diversity means happiness between cultures, color, and

gender.

Start in your heart then go to your mind, start with love to

show that you're kind. There is love in diversity. In our

difference we find happiness, only then are we the same.

We Are All The Same

We are all the same, and yet we're different,

From dust we came, we are all heaven sent,

Divine purpose, to unify and restore,

What happened to us?

The Lord knocks, open the door,

Why are we this way?

We bath in blood,

Why do you stay?

Our hearts are gone and done,

Crosses still burn at the barrel of our guns,

We've turned to stone,

Prejudice thinks it won

Why think we can kill to make it to another day?

Knowledge is power, we can change our fate,

Unnecessary deaths, the force of our will,

Trayvon Martin, Emmett Till,

Do you understand?

Can you hear their screams?

"Don't shed tears over us,

Live out our dreams"

Don't forget the past,

Create a new future,

We all came from the same place,

Restore the suture,

From dust we came, and to dust we will return,

We're all the same shade, we all must learn,

The wages of sin is death, and so it must be,

The question remains,

Where will you spend eternity?

American Dream, American Freedom

Who wants the war? Who wants the peace?

Who wants the bonds to break and cease?

Who wants the dream to finally come true?

Who wants the freedom to do what you want to do?

Who did all the fighting? Who just relaxed?

What's even the reason? Is it the tax?

The blood and tears of men and women, trying to get rid

of their fears, so they can keep on living.

Do we just stand and watch? And listen to the clocks go

tick and tock.

They killed the women, they killed the children, and they

burned the houses in which they were living.

Their dreams were not shattered, they live through us, the

sons and daughters of their American dream.

And their hope for American freedom. But who says it's over, who says it's done?

There's a lot to do before we can say that we've won.

The soldiers are out there, with their lives flashing before them.

They didn't care that they might die, they just cared for the lives of their friends, and not for the lies of their enemy.

Thanks to their faith and determination, we were able to win, and build our great nation.

Thanks to their American dream, we have American freedom.

Burning Night

When the windows start to open and close,

And nobody knows that something is hissing,

What would happen to them nobody knows,

For they know not what they are missing,

Then a bang was heard in the night air,

Loud enough to make all time stand still,

The houses were burning without care,

With a smell so bad, it can make you ill,

The screams not heard,

The people not seen,

Kids trying to get through the herd,

The world knows not what this might mean,

They just stand and watch,

While their house is ablaze,

Burning through the crotch,

Kids running through a burning maze,

Born into heartbreak,

The baby screams,

The earth begins to quake,

Nothing is what it seems,

No one sees what lies ahead,

You cover your eyes,

All the family is dead,

The kids will never again see their room,

Yet they are reminded of this night's doom,

Sadness

I've lost all I loved, everyone I hurt

I'm through with suffering

Can I return to the earth?

Dust I came, dust I shall leave

No more will my touch cause sadness to weave

I'm through, I'm done, I've given up

No matter what I say, it's not enough

I'll not be missed, no tear shall be shed

The world will smile...once I'm dead

I wanted to give all I had

But that you would not take

I was just a trophy

And my heart you would rake

Wonder why life torments me so...

Soon it'll not be my worry

To the grave I go.

For the Love of God

There is silence...in the world

All except for the tears of a girl

Hear her cry, hear her scream

Watch her tear at the seams

It's a never-ending cycle of pain.

For the love of God

Let this end

Can we ever go back where there's peace again?

For the love of God

Now we cry

Can't we all just be able to rise?

There is violence...in your heart

Blood is thicker than water

But we're still far apart

The air is thick...with smoke

The flames are rising

What are we doing, what are we doing

For the love of God

Let this end

Can we ever go back where there's peace again?

For the love of God

Now we cry

Can't we all just be able to rise?

What have we done

How much longer til the victory is won?

How much longer do we cry?

Life goes on...by and by

Bittersweet

Was the world always so bittersweet?

Walking down the street I see more than I should see,

Children, thrown like footballs but never land in the end

zone...abandoned...dying slowly,

Blood splattered like red wings, trying to set the soul

free...dark angels,

I'm tired of watching our kids struggle and have to raise

themselves because adults can't lead by example,

What's wrong with us?

Young girls getting pregnant, young girls getting married,

Can you picture that?

A baby raising another baby,

The world nowadays is so bittersweet,

Sweat and work all day just to be shot during the week,

I shouldn't have to wear a bulletproof vest to attempt to

live happily,

What is justice? What is peace?

Life and liberty, it's just for the deceased

We the people, dead and gone, wish the living to live on,

Walk down the street and see harmony,

Love thy neighbor, quit all the complaitin',

If y'all didn't know that's complaining and hating,

Something's wrong with us

Earth should be renamed to Wormwood,

So bitter we can barely live,

We're choking on our own poison,

Quick, yet slow torture,

Killing me softly yet rough,

And we can't get enough,

Well maybe you can't, but I can,

The world is still so bittersweet,

And until we can find peace for eternity,

Y'all can keep the bitter,

I'll keep the sweet.

Silence is Louder than Words

"You have the right to remain silent"
One of the rights we seem to have,
Raped...in silence.
Scarred...in silence.
For once I want my rights to silence taken away,
Thrown away.
Take the muzzle off my mouth so I can speak,
Let me have my voice back.
"Anything you say can and will be held against you"
Held against me?
You were the one who held me.
And you have the nerve to say that slavery is over,
That we've evolved, that we've moved on.
Think again.
You are my new chains.
Look at my face, look what you've done.
Haven't even started the race you've claimed that you
won.
Your court of law may save you now...

But you have a higher court to answer to later.

Forced to remain silent, so I said this with my eyes.

The one part that saw through your lies.

Through it all, I know I was heard,

Silence is louder than words.

<u>Poetic Strength</u>

"Leadership and strength are one and the same.
One cannot be without the other. We are all
natural leaders, born with strength. Our lives
gives us the additional strength to endure, so
that we may lead others to do what is right."
-Poetic Melodies

Leadership

The leaders of today
Or at least that's what they say
But are they really leaders at all
They know the difference of right and wrong
Yet they aren't afraid to help you fall
The new leaders of tomorrow
Or at least that's what we hear
Seem to have plenty to fear
To follow the leaders of nothings galore
And try to be something more
The leaders of our future
And I'm not afraid to say
They'll pave the way
And fix our mistakes
"And a child shall lead them"
They've got what it takes
So take care and educate
So the wrong leaders won't be
Masters of your fate

Crazy in Youth

Crazy

I must be crazy

Crazy in youth

Nothing lasts forever

Can time stop just for me?

I want to be young forever

The youngest leader in eternity

So maybe I am crazy

Crazy in my youth

That I created from

The fairytales I claimed I hated

Purifying the communities

That say they can't relate

Crazy

I really must be crazy

To try and make my dreams a reality

To fly higher than the highest tree

Can time stop just for me?

I can save a life

Climb the greatest mountains

Protest for my freedom

Design magnificent fountains

Crazy I am

Crazy I shall be

When my time stops

I'll be youth eternally

Groovin' High

Pick up your feet across the floor,

Tonight we're gonna fly,

Time stops just for me,

I'm never gonna die,

All our cares fade away,

Bumping with the music and the beat,

Our skin is black and brown and wheat,

All racism is on the street,

Swing! Swing!

Our skirts fling,

We finally have some fun,

Dance til the moon touches the sun.

Guess What?

Guess what? Today I'm 17, and I'm rushing home.

My parents said they had a surprise for me, and I can't wait!

I wonder what it is...

Guess what? When I got home, there was no one there.

I waited for someone to turn on the lights and scream, "Surprise!"

Guess what? It never came. That one birthday turned to many days. I sat and waited for the people to come out and say, "You punk'd!"

But they never came.

I am now 25 and completely alone. Too many bills, not enough money, now I'm without a home.

Guess what? You disappeared off the face of the earth, but I dream about you everyday as if you were right next to me.

Rehab wasn't so bad, but therapy was the worst. They tried to say you guys didn't exist, so I put them under a curse.

Oops. It didn't work anyway.

Guess what? An all-white room, a straitjacket, and unbreakable glass is not how I like to spend a Christmas. So when my soul is finally laid to rest, and I stand before the gates.

One push...and down you fell to meet your fate.

Guess what? Even though you descended down, I tried to wish you well. But as I walked through the gates of heaven, you went straight to hell.

Poetic Passion

"Love, lust, and passion...emotions so strong it can make you write the most powerful pieces. Earth shattering vows made into tidal waves crashing into the hearts of man." - Poetic Melodies

Love

Learning from the person you love

Overcoming all the hate that comes at you

Vowing to love forever

Everlasting marriage

For My Love

My love for you is true

We could bring eternity to its knees

For no one made me feel like this but you

I feel higher than the trees

You bring the light to my darkness

You are my sun

You warm me like no other

You are my only one

We will live this life

And five more before we are done

I will be your wife

Together we are one

Dreaming of You

When I'm lying in my bed,

With the pillow underneath my head,

I start to close my eyes and dream of you,

When I'm lost, you helped me find the truth,

When I'm blind, you were there to see me through,

When I'm sad, you were there to comfort me,

And for that I'll always love you,

Everytime, I look into your eyes,

I see the love that makes me want to fly,

You can feel my heart beating fast,

When I'm dreaming of you.

Prince of My Heart

You're everything I hoped for
Before it was just a dream
Now that I have you by my side
It's become a reality
My love for you is endless
And though we have our struggles
I still consider you my prince
And the feelings in our cuddles
You're everything I need and more
And though right now we may be temporarily apart
You'll always be the prince of my heart

Eternal

Once I felt,

The love that I imagined,

But my heart grew dark,

And I turned away,

But now that I look,

I start to realize,

That the love is eternal,

And I should've stayed,

My life is turning black,

I had to face the facts,

That I can't do anything without you,

Now I know the wrong in my ways,

Without you I am nothing.

What can I do?

Can I come back to you?

Can you make me whole?

You have the love I've been searching for,

Can you make me whole?

I Do

One day, I felt joy

But I was confused.

My perfect boy,

Had me misused.

Sitting in my shame,

I've lost my name,

With a broken heart,

I can't explain,

What could I do,

With those three words,

"I love you,"

Floating in the air,

Who could take me there,

I need you,

I do

I am much more than a doormat,

The walking on me is through,

What ever happened,

To when we said, "I do"

What ever happened to our love,

I'm looking up above,

Nothing can compare,

How do we fare,

What is there to do,

With those two words,

"I do"

What's The Point?

What's the point of trying to love?

What's the big deal of having feelings?

For someone that is unreal?

What's the love that you've been trying to find?

Who can help you?

Can your heart see what you see?

Will your mind think what you feel?

Will you let love live toward your mind?

The thump of your heart will show,

That you know your time has come.

Love will find your way no matter,

If you get thinner or you get fatter.

Then your heart gets broken one more time.

And all you can think or say is... "What's the point?!"

I've Been Thinking

I've been thinking...

I can't take it anymore

You say you'll change

You say it'll get better

So why am I feeling trapped?

I've been thinking...

Nothing I do seems to please you

No matter how many times

I say I love you

You don't trust a word I say.

I've been thinking...

Love can't live where there's no trust

And ours is dying rapidly

No medical procedure can save us.

I've been thinking...

You don't pay me attention anymore

You're either too busy or too tired to talk

But you can party and play games with your "sistahs"

And let's not forget the bros.

I've been thinking...

If you didn't want to be with me

Why didn't you just say so?

Why leave me in the dark?

Am I just for show?

I've been thinking...

When you show my pictures

You secretly like hearing all the compliments of my outer

beauty

Just because you never saw the inner

I've been thinking...

There's no us anymore

It's just you

It's just me

I've been thinking...

It's time for us to end.

High School Heartbreak

Freshman year: we meet in class,

You all shy, guys trying to get in my pants,

I tried to approach you, but was intercepted,

They didn't want my kind around you to be accepted,

And then I was stripped of all of my virtue,

My dignity taken, rumors were thought true,

No one tried to help me, even you believed the lies,

But I still loved you by and by,

Sophomore year: more like solitary confinement,

I was all alone, while you shined like diamonds,

Stuck in the library, I thought I made a friend,

We then formed a triangle, with you no where to be my
real friend,

Off and on I cried my tears, but with no one to cry to...

It was the hardest second year,

Rumors kept spreading like wildfire,

I still had hope, but I was tired,

Junior year: don't make me remember,

We had class together again, but it was more like torture,

It was like freshman year all over again,

Except there was no penetration, God was looking out for me then,

The fire continues, no one can stop the lies,

I looked to you with hope in my eyes,

But your "friends" turned you away from me, calling me "easy",

If you looked at me closely, that was all I could never be,

Senior year: it's almost over,

The war's almost finished, I've been a good soldier,

We had each other in class again, I had no hope you'd look my way,

To my surprise, we got together, the sun was shining my way,

We had our arguments and of course more happiness,

My only regret is that when you gave me your virtue, I couldn't give mine to you back,

We loved each other, at least that's what we said,

Pretty words to carry when we're dead,

Graduation day: finally!

From the chains of high school, now we're free,

You kissed me as everyone threw their caps in the air,

Balloons and flowers everywhere,

That night we were together, I slept in your arms,

Convinced we'd be together, I should've felt some alarm,

We parted ways for that day only, and for all summer we

met,

For our share of glory,

Summertime: we shared every bit of the sun,

I looked in your eyes and I thought I was the only one,

Your kisses were soft, like the breast of a dove,

I wanted to continue that sweet love,

You held me in your arms, I wanted time to stop forever,

To continue that feeling, hotter than the weather,

We swore to be together, that was just the beginning,

Who knew it'd be the beginning to an ending,

College, freshman year: here we go again,

We had class together, but this one was different,

All you had to do was touch me and I was overtaken,

You were my angel, I thought I was in heaven,

I was falling hard, but you never caught me,

I hit the ground hard, bruised all over me,

Before the next summer, together we will be,

At least the inner me was hoping,

Summertime: summer classes,

As complex as my love life, pining away, wishing to be your wife,

We tried to be together again but you had feelings for another,

Instead of telling me the truth, you start a fight over nothing,

You looked so cold when I tried to hug you,

Just one touch and you froze like an icicle,

You were looking for a reason, you never wanted to give me a chance,

I just made you feel good, you lead the heartbreak dance,

Classes embark: I'm supposed to look happy,

But looks are deceiving, I found that firsthand,

You were my light in my darkness that I called life,

Like a star I was never meant to touch,

I come closer to the light, which is nothing more than a fire,

Now extinguished, not even smoke rises,

You left me to die, in the coldness of despair,

But I wish you every happiness, I'll never be there,

The memories come rolling, my heart starts to ache,

My life will constantly be just like high school,

Heartbreak.

Say Goodbye

Went through hell and high water
I came back crushed
Devastated
I suppose I expected too much
From a man who says he loves me
Then leaves in a cruel world to fight
I wanted the love of my father
Turning darkness to light
You are the incarnate of my fears
The embodiment of my shame
Just another demon
To add after my name
You think you can have me
After all that's done and said
You'll have to get over it
I'm sleeping peacefully in bed
I want love
But if wanted you
I'd want despair

And so to have my peace

I'll let my Peacemaker keep me

To get through my Armor

Impossible task

Say goodbye to all of your masks

I think I know

I think I know
I made the mistakes
I think I understand
Your heart was torn apart with a fine toothed rake
But it wasn't just me
You played your part
You too raked over my heart
And now I suffer
Longing to be free
Can I ever go back to the way I used to be
You changed me
Was it for the better or worse
I never know from the way you would curse
I always made you angry
I always felt useless
The tears I cry
Can't handle the abuses
Mishandled, abused, ripped apart, used, misunderstood,
depressed

When will I find rest
You moved on from me
But I stayed in place
I don't think I can finish this race
So while you get your happiness
I'll eat your dust
While I'm wishing for your touch
I wish you well
I know you'll be grand
I think I know
I think I understand

Enigma

I really don't know what I feel
Love, depression
Both are real
I feel lower than the dust
The tears I cry only make me rust
You'll never understand
You hurt me in a way that no other man can
But I can't live without you
What a fool I am
Falling for someone that fell out with me
Am I really that desperate? Said my insecurities
Truth is I am desperate
You were all I had
You became a vital part of my living
Someone I want to have
I did not give my consent
There is no exchange
No man can replace you
My love can't change

Emotion is something I tried to avoid

But you came along and made me vulnerable

I was your moldable toy

You don't understand

And neither do I

My feelings are an enigma

Unsolvable mysteries of a feeble mind

So the tears I shed now

I'll shed forever

Wishing

Wishing

Wishing

For my always and forever

Dear Whoever,

I know you can see this, so I'm going to make this quick.

I wonder, can you do a magic trick?

You try to preach about all of these fears...

But, tell me, can you make these fears disappear?

When you get this letter, I hope you can see...

Every letter is filled with insecurities.

Do you think that maybe I have low self-esteem?

Do you think it's still possible for me to dream?

Maybe you can reply, since you're so holy...

Sincerely Yours,

My name is Lonely

Poetic Healing

"The foundation of the heart can be quite shaky, but when set on the path of righteousness, even an earthquake can't reach it." -Poetic Melodies

Freedom

Freedom is the hope of the slave, while we work and not
get paid,

they're down at another part of the field whipping a slave.

Africa, my homeland, they stole it from me,

and then they whip me because I want to be free.

Freedom is what we ask for, to be free under God's sun

any time, any day.

We don't get freedom; instead we get beat,

and then get back in the hot summer heat.

Four hundred years we've waited, for God to end it all,

and to give us our freedom, that's all we ask for.

Then President Lincoln's law went out, now we don't

work for free.

Now we go from the plantations cheerfully.

Freedom is the hope of the slave, and we got freedom.

Finally. Now we can say, "Free at last! Free at last! Thank

God Almighty, we're free at last!"

Alone But Not Lonely

Did you ever think about the times when,

you thought you really had some friends?

You were like a pedestal, body made of stone,

this is what it's like when you're feeling alone.

You used to think the world's coming to an end,

while you're searching for that one true friend.

You were wanting someone to take this loneliness away,

one to keep you from falling and wouldn't send you away.

That one true friend is Jesus, you see.

He is always with you, so you will never be lonely.

To think that at one point, life was coming to an end,

now you found your one true friend,

who'll help you begin.

He's always there, so call Him, not by phone.

Call Him with your heart,

and you'll know you're not alone.

Sometimes you feel happy, sometimes you'll feel sad.

Sometimes you'll feel angry, sometimes you'll feel blue.

But you'll never feel alone, because Jesus is there with you.

You may feel alone, but you'll never be lonely.

Love and Hate

What's with all this love and hate?

Stop all the fighting, let's celebrate!

People all over dying with fear,

but their hearts are busy saying, "Hello is someone here?"

God doesn't like all this fighting and tears,

He sent Jesus here to get rid of our fear.

People don't believe what they've got inside,

God's love is waiting, it doesn't want to hide.

But buried under that love is whole bunch of hate,

and then the love fades away like dust on a plate.

How can you be someone who loves to hate or hates to be

loved?

You can be both of these things and still be loved.

Do you know who it is? Is it the Devil?

No! He loves to hate. That leaves one left, and that's Jesus.

Jesus will love you, even when you're hated by other people around you.

Love to be loved, hate to be hated.

Spend all your time loving so you won't get into Hades.

There is two hearts, but only one love.

Yearn to love, and Jesus will come running.

Poetic Eternity

"The way to happiness is a difficult one, but when you find the strength to carry on despite the weight of the world's burdens, eternity will be within your reach." –Poetic Melodies

Jesus

Jumping to help when you're in need

Evolving into whatever you need

Sacrificing His life to save yours

United with the Father to help you stand

Staying in heaven holding your hands

Jesus Christ

Joy during a rough time can

Equal to peace, like you've never had

Salvation brought back to

Us using the love and mercy of our

Savior Jesus

Christ, a king of kings

He lives in our hearts

Real in our souls,

In our minds

Salvation came

To save us all

Just Imagine

Close your eyes, open your mind,

Just try to imagine, what you try to find,

Listen with your heart, listen with your soul,

Create the feeling that helps your goal,

Many may try to see what's on your mind,

But they don't understand what they're trying to find,

They say to take that leap of faith,

But can't seem to remember your name...

Just imagine the one that you seek,

Will you find them on top a mountain peak?

Just imagine that maybe you could be...

The one with no insecurities?

Do you think that you can imagine when you meet your

end?

Do you have a family? Do you have a friend?

Can you live through the infinite space?

Can you make it to the end of the race?

So if you can imagine,

Move forward, not behind...

That you can set out and seek what you find

Find and Believe

To find the key you have to find the lock,

to find the lock you have to find the door,

to find the door you have to find the heart,

to find the heart you have to find the soul,

to find the soul you have to find the spirit,

to find the spirit you have to find Jesus,

to find Jesus you have to believe.

What does this mean to you?

What should this mean to you?

Search for Him,

Call His Name,

He will answer.

Magic

Ladies and Gentlemen, boys and girls,

Let's get ready for your curls to unfurl,

What I will tell will create shivers down your spine,

Now who can tell the one true time?

Of destruction and creation,

Grace and salvation,

Beginning and the end,

Demons and friends,

Angels and liars,

Laughers and criers,

Heaven and Hell,

Now who can really tell?

Now let us bring truth to light,

Look at your heart and get yourself right,

Now you don't know,

The end may be tragic,

It's time for the show,

Poof! It's magic.

Voices

Who is that? Who's there?

Why are you talking? Why do you care?

I hear you, but why should I listen?

It's not like you're here, you're dead.

I'm sorry, you've risen.

I hear your voice, so soft, yet so clear.

It makes me feel like you were always right here.

I've been through so much hurt.

I've been through so much pain.

Can you heal my heart, Oh Lamb that was slain?

Show me the true way, give me direction.

Not just a piece of a section.

Every word you say comes out crystal clear.

Why, oh, why did I choose not to hear?

You helped me get rid of all that I fear

Now I'm crying joyous tears

Thank you, oh voices, that spoke to me.

Now I lift my praises to thee.

Now all you other people, put out your ear.

Shh...listen, the Lord is near

Standing

I've been scarred

Abused

I've been lied on

Misused

I've been treated like I'm less than dust

I've been bagged on

Bruised

I've been ragged on

And I'd lose

I've been treated like I'm less than dust

But I'm still standing

I'm still standing

I've got both feet onto the ground

I'm still standing

I am standing

I'm still standing

And nobody's gonna bring me down

I've been treated like I'm less than dust

I've been treated like a metal gone to rust

I'm still standing

Still standing

Peace Be Still

Bring light, bring peace

Bring goodness, bring sleep

Let joy be awakened

Let no person be forsakened

Bring quiet, bring smiles

So that our hearts won't turn so vile

Let peace be still

Let God do as He will

Enough of the screaming

Enough of the fighting

Enough of the yelling

Enough of the rioting

Bring quiet, bring smiles

So that our hearts won't be so vile

Bring light, bring peace

Bring goodness, bring sleep

Let peace be still

Let God do as He will

Let joy be awakened

Let no person be forsakened

Let peace be still

Peace be still

Game Over

Welcome to the end of the game.

It seems you have won the title-name.

But wait, do I see the ultimate high score?

You must have it, no you must have more!

One life left, the game seems to say.

But you venture on anyway.

You're fingers rush against the controller.

Your back soon feels like you've been hit with a boulder.

Through the trials of the game you must go.

By a thin line your faith lingers so.

Then with one final snap the thread begins to break.

You lose all trust, your fingers start to shake.

Your confidence is shattered, your self esteem battered.

Your last life is gone, but you wish to live on.

Then that message flashes across the screen...

Game Over.

It's done, you've lost, they've won.

Life, Knowledge, Addiction

My life was spent in a library.

Losing myself in the sanctity, while also losing my sanity.

Gorging myself with the fiction and nonfiction.

Mistaking the difference between reality and infinite
energy.

Knowledge is the key to life, and reading is fundamental.

And since knowledge holds it's own vitality, I'll become a
vampire.

Sucking the blood of knowledge from the spines of the
books, gaining new strength,

Because knowledge is power.

It makes me wonder if leaders, both old and new, ever
took the time to pick up a book.

If they did, they would probably understand that wars are
created from unnecessary bloodshed,

Families and allies turning on each other like it's World
War II, and that sometimes people will do anything to get
to a throne.

They want something or someone to own, but their bookshelves are bare.

More people need to read, because the potency of illiteracy is stronger than any drug.

It's an addiction that's more welcome than getting on to crack cocaine.

Stronger than any alcohol, but sweeter, too.

Get addicted to reading.

Break the chains of ignorance and stupidity that has been on your shoulders.

Weighing you down like 13 tons underwater.

Suffocating.

You're struggling.

You need to breathe.

You need knowledge.

Believe, Dream, Imagine

Love all you can

And when you don't get it back

Don't get discouraged

For everyone still has to

Love themselves before anyone

Else loves them

Giving love doesn't mean that it's

Given back to you

Trust that your love will bring

Happiness to everyone around you

And that's all the love you need

Author's Note

Thank you for reading this book. These poems are based on my past experiences and dreams that I have had. I hope you enjoyed reading these poems as much as I enjoyed writing them. These poems mean very much to me, and I am very glad to share my work with the world. I hope you enjoyed the lessons behind each poem. I learned a lot, and I hope you did, too!

Charity "Poetic Melodies" Crawford

99313311R00052

Made in the USA
Columbia, SC
08 July 2018